AND

IT CAME

TO PASS

IN THE OLD TESTAMENT

By Eric Scott

42 BIBLE STORIES FOR GROWN-UPS

And It Came To Pass
In The Old Testament:
42 Bible Stories for Grown-Ups

ISBN-13: 978-0-9981829-5-7

Printed in the United States of America

RevMedia Publishing

PO BOX 5172, Kingwood, TX 77325

Unless otherwise noted, all Scripture references are taken from
the King James Version Bible. Used by permission.

Forward

For years I have enjoyed studying and teaching the Bible, as a lay person, a professional theologian, and now as a lay person again. After obtaining degrees in biology and business administration at major universities I launched a career in swimming pool water purification. My work at two Fortune 100 corporations led me to become CEO of a small chemical manufacturing company. Having been deeply involved in local churches most of my life I sensed a spiritual calling and enrolled in one of America's most renowned seminaries as a middle-aged businessman with a family of four.

I have pastored churches, visited excavated sites in the Holy Land, led seminars, preached in stadiums, and attended hundreds of church related events rubbing elbows with people of virtually every Christian denomination. After years of studying and lecturing I no longer count myself an expert on the Bible. I am now simply another humbled seeker. I remain on a spiritual quest though I am no longer a religious institutionalist. Some who read this will relate.

My wife and I invested our retirement funds in a small restaurant where I never tire of mixing with smart people who may, or may not, share my Christian perspective. I particularly like to spar with intelligent, well-educated people of diverse backgrounds over contentious religious matters and controversial current events. I have discovered that decent people can enjoy sincere well-founded dialog and grow from each other's genuine peculiar beliefs. Iron sharpens iron according to an insightful proverb.

I am greatly encouraged by how interested people I engage with are about spiritual issues. However, I'm amazed at how ignorant most folks are about the Bible, itself. I find it amusing, though somewhat annoying, how dogmatic some individuals can be about their particular religious views, and how quickly they become put off by someone else's genuinely held beliefs, or lack thereof. Dogmatism and naivety both kill dialog, and one of my greatest concerns is for people who have developed a jaundiced view of the Bible, organized religion, or even God, based on what they've observed in others who say they're Christian.

Sadly today, capable persuasive secular antagonists twist science and alter history in a relentless quest to discredit the Bible. I still think of science as an objective pursuit of reality, though much of what's parleyed as science today is actually little more than the promotion of an unresolved agendas from various vested positions. On issues ranging from world climate to a healthy personal diet, too many of us are painstakingly diligent about spreading our biased misinformation. The same holds true in religious thought. There is a difference between constructive debate and self-seeking manipulation.

And It Came To Pass is a simple overview of the Bible based on my understanding with a lot of input from various sources over many years of study. I happen to believe the stories in this book, but they are filtered through my own experience and analysis. Hopefully, my unconventional rendering of these familiar stories will provide fresh insight for your next religious conversation. This project is not authorized by any party or group. My conclusions are not documented or sourced. The stories are abbreviated and abridged for the sake of expedience and concision. Scripture quotations are from the Authorized King James translation of the Holy Bible or my own rendering of it. I hope this book makes you reflect on what you believe and why you believe a particular way.

The Holy Bible is a single story composed of 66 books. The Old Testament consist of 39 books and covers the period from man's beginnings, or genesis, to the period around 400 BC when sacred Jewish history went silent. The 27 books in the New Testament address the life of Jesus of Nazareth and the establishment of the Christian Church. I have broken this project into two parts to make it more manageable for readers, but the two are inseparably linked. It doesn't matter where you start or what stories you are attracted to, but realize that all the stories together make a single story that is the essence of the Holy Bible. I included a couple of inter-testament period stories in the latter book to synthesize the two and fill in some needed information. May this effort bless your life, as my quest to understand and explain the sacred Holy Bible blesses mine.

Table of Contents

Prelude

It seems the Holy Bible isn't revered as it once was. Efforts to have it shunned or even legally banned from the public arena have been largely successful. Many young people today have had little or no exposure to it. You can attend a variety of churches and never come to really know their foundational document. Those who are familiar with fundamental Scriptures too seldom engage in pursuits that expand their comprehension or engrain biblical precepts into their constitution.

Even children can gain from exposure to the Bible's moral tenets, but it's not a quick easy read. Because it contains colorful characters and dynamic events that relate to our history and Earth's geography, watered down accounts provide fun reading matter for kids at bedtime. And It Came To Pass In The Old Testament is a resource for serious adults who have a good idea what the Bible is about, but may question its validity, premise, significance, relevance or importance. If the Bible is what it clearly purports to be, it should be taken very seriously.

Much of what is contained in these Bible-based stories won't jive with some common notions. You won't see Noah as a reclusive hermit chopping and dragging trees to make a huge boat, chasing tigers with a rope, or luring elephants with a basket of peanuts. You won't find Moses herding millions of slaves from Egypt like scared mice feverishly sprinting across a dry riverbed between two thirty-foot walls of raging water.

You will envision Bible characters as real people and epoch stories as legitimate events. You'll come to appreciate that each person and every event is recorded for a purpose. There were miracles to be sure, though you may not know how to fully assimilate them. You will learn to bite off what you can chew, chew what you can swallow, and swallow what you can digest. As Jesus used to teach, you become the words and thoughts you consume.

If you read this book all the way through and follow it up with research at a library or on the internet, you will see that the Bible is a lot more relevant and believable than you might have previously thought. In fact, you'll find that the Bible is intellectually dependable and offers feasible answers to questions that really matter. When you learn to decipher the mysteries that are shrouded in plain sight, you'll begin to connect dots that bring order and purpose to your life and man's existence on Earth.

Aside from gaining a better scientific and historical perspective, you'll also begin to realize why Jews and Palestinians contend for the same territory they've been disputing for thousands of years; why Jews, and Christians by extension, believe their God is unique; why Jews and Muslims don't easily convert to Christianity; and why sincere Christians can't compromise on controversial social matters they deem crucial to their faith. The aim is to open closed minds to explore viable probabilities.

Some people dogmatically insist the words in their particular translation of the Bible are to be interpreted verbatim. Unfortunately, most folks who hold that view don't benefit from a working knowledge of the original languages and cultures from which the text was derived. Some hold the view that the Bible is a collection of useful illustrations and allegories that various ancient writers were mysteriously inspired to record for mankind's eventual discovery. They rationalize and intellectualize the sacred text into total impotence. If you dissect a living body you gain insights about its structure, but you forfeit what gave it life.

Of course, there are those who dismiss the Bible as a bundle of fantastic myths and fables written by ambitious imposters and gathered by manipulative clerics to impose their worldview on ignorant underlings. The Bible recognizes all points of view, declaring, "Every man is right in his own eyes." The premise of the Bible is that it doesn't matter what you think. Truth is truth whether we recognize it, understand it, and accept it, or not. The Bible accommodates every opinion proposing that, "Now we see the world through murky glass. Only when we shed our physical trappings will we see things as they really are."

The Bible is so intricate and complex it couldn't be fully mastered by the most intelligent scholar in an extended lifetime of study. Yet, it's so simple that children are able to comprehend its essential tenets. The Bible is "milk for babes in faith, and meat for those who have grown to digest it." This book extrapolates essential elements into short stories about selected people, topics, and events that are widely known, sometimes disputed, and often misunderstood. When you question something, just keep reading. The stories come together and make sense when they converge in the end.

Every chapter of this book is designed to be an independent story, so you can pick and choose what you would like to read by topic according to your interests. However, it is designed to unfold chronologically and help establish a rational perspective from a 21st century biblical worldview. The whole is greater than the sum of its parts. Try not to get bogged down or diverted by questionable details until you see and can follow the master plan. Please allow me to open a window and shed new light from a different angle that might help you see more clearly some important biblical nuances you may have overlooked.

Part 1

The Patriarchal Age

1

In The Beginning

Everything that exists had to come from something somewhere at some time. Finding what the first thing came from and where that was and when it happened is the greatest mystery of all. Without time, force, energy, space and matter nothing in our world could exist. These are essential parameters and everything exists within their purview. They allow for all we know and measure in our material world. They govern the operation of science, math, art and every natural physical endeavor.

Imagine no form, pattern, purpose, plan or destiny. Secular science aligns with the Holy Bible at this critical juncture. In a brilliant flash, a genuine big bang, something beyond the realm of vast emptiness started a process that has unfolded into the ordered structure all around us. The Bible proclaims that, "In the beginning (time), God (a force) created (energy) the heavens (space) and the earth (matter)." Then, having very succinctly delineated the foundation for every law of physics, chemistry, and mathematics, including laws of relativity, thermodynamics and even the rudiments of evolution, the Bible advances the idea that over a series of six epoch spans the giant universe expanded from a tiny object of deified thought to an unfathomable world of irrefutable realities.

Once upon a time long ago, an idea became manifested in reality. Like a storyteller unveiling his genius and making his inner thoughts and plans come to life, God spoke his tale into existence. We are simply living out his story. If that's true, the author would have known the end from the beginning. The entire storyline and outcome were established before the proverbial book of life was published. That concept, and our understanding and participation, will loom large as we turn pages and look for answers to questions that serve to determine our fate and expose our course and destiny.

First, an explosion of rays and waves projected from a compressed seed of raw energy. It filled the void and expanded the borders of space in all directions. What we know as light, even outside our perceptible spectrum, roared across the universe uninhibited and unabated. The empty silent darkness could not resist it. The event and its immediate aftermath could not have been measured in our simple ohms and decibels and degrees. Nothing we know could have survived such a blast.

In a universe still expanding at the speed of light, raw energy eventually collided and congealed into superhot masses that stretched like fresh warm taffy and formed terrestrial bodies that acted in accordance with the same scientific laws that govern the small galaxy we occupy today. Generally speaking, $E=MC^2$; energy converts to mass at an equivalent determinable rate, constantly striving toward thermal equilibrium. Scientifically speaking, everything that exists has existed in some form since what we know as "existence" began.

The second era particular to the world we know and live in was occasioned when hot masses began to separate and cool. Layers formed in accordance to their temperature and density in compliance with gravity and centrifugal force created by the electrolytic attraction of swirling chemical elements that, as far as we can tell, constitute every object in space. The Bible declares in that day firmaments or strata enveloped the object we call Earth as molecules developed and stabilized, driven by their atomic attraction and corresponding molecular weights.

What began as a student project less than a decade ago, measuring atmospheric gases captured in what were heralded as 2.7 billion year old meteor fragments extracted from limestone found in western Australia, has become a major government funded research endeavor. According to science, it appears that Earth, uniquely composed of large quantities of hydrogen and oxygen, as well as carbon and nitrogen, was perhaps once encased by an outer shell of ice where steamy mist rose to meet frozen space. As the molten mass we call land broke through the liquid mass we call seas, it cooled and hardened. It yielded vegetation like a virtual terrarium and each life form that appeared was able to replicate and regenerate after its own kind. In the Book of Genesis the Bible calls that period the third day.

As the sky cleared and our solar system stabilized, celestial bodies then many light-years away appeared and assumed routine dependable rotations and patterns of movement that must have been very similar to what we postulate by observation today. At last, our sun appeared and a day could really be called a day. A near equivalent darkness allowed for viewing our moon and the countless stars, though no eyes were yet there to see them. Oddly, the Bible asserts the story of God's handiwork was written in the heavens and was visible from Earth even on that fourth day. From beginning to end, the story of our occupation, though beyond our full comprehension, was already established and set in our stars.

When the physics and the temperature were right and the chemical balance was suitable, the Bible says God brought forth life cultivated from the sea. Over the course of that epoch long fifth day, every creature was established by what we now call its chromosomes. The genetic field was complete and able to yield any species or genre of any plant or animal that could eventually come into existence. Creatures made their way onto the land and soared into the sky and occupied spaces and climates well suited for them.

In the sixth period of creation the animal kingdom flourished and continued to change in what seems to have been a hyperbaric tropical paradise. God determined to make mankind after his own likeness, though surely not his physical likeness because God is beyond physical definition. Among the other beings He created, God made man, a willful creature with a distinct moral awareness. Man alone was able to create, and conscious of his creator.

God vested the stewardship of Earth in mankind. Man would be accountable to God for the well-being of every life form and natural habitat in the vast, self-sustaining garden. It seems from the text, the first creatures were vegetarian and there was ample fruit for all. Or at least the entire food chain was based on vegetation as we know to be true today. God decreed that both beast and man could devour as much as they desired from any of the abundant life sources He provided. Everything was perfect and balanced, and God looked upon what he had done and said it was very good. Then He retired from his labors, creating nothing new, nothing more from nothing, in the historical era, or what we might call the seventh day.

2

God Made Man

I t's scientifically most plausible that a force outside our universe initiated our existence. That's because all natural laws preclude an entity creating itself from nothing, and it's hard to refute all natural laws with science. Before time, space, matter, and energy existed, a force beyond our reasoning could have done it. The Bible says it did. The Bible calls that force God. So whether you call that pre-existing force God or not, we are talking about the same thing. Because that thing preceded time and space and matter we can't define what it is or where it is or when it started. But it still exists, and we can only understand it in terms of our space-time perspective.

The Bible does not pose itself as a science text. However, it divulges scientific nuggets and does not refute the natural laws it purports to have initiated. Those conflicts come from assumptions and interpretations that take the original text where it does not necessarily go. The Bible is not a history text. It chronicles events, but not always in detail or time order.

The Bible simply submits that mankind was created in conformance with laws of science and the will of the force that initiated our existence. Using the laws of science and natural order to analyze our beginning, several models emerge. None can be replicated so none can be confirmed. The "big bang" is pretty well agreed upon with modest variations. Those who adhere to the Bible look beyond the impotent assumption that it was a random spontaneous event. The sequences leading from the bang to the present follow a logical and mandatory scientific order. Three points that breach natural protocol are the creation itself, the appearance of life, and the emergence of intelligence.

The first two chapters of the Bible introduce three mysteries it later addresses in more detail. First, the Bible focuses on the Earth, as though the creation of the entire universe was merely accommodation for a habitable planet. The existence of other worlds is apparent, but the Bible is a book about Earth. It even allows for what we categorize as paranormal activity, suggesting we cannot fully apprehend it and ought not immerse ourselves in what is beyond our understanding and out of our control.

Second, a physical Earth was encased by firmaments that made it appear and operate like a giant layered bubble in space. The temperature of cosmic space is minus 455 degrees Fahrenheit. Earth is now 10,800 degrees at its center. Earth is unique among all known planets in its material composition. Abundant life supporting elemental gasses rose as vapors from a boiling surface to the edge of space. There they would have formed a layer of ice that encased a layer of steam which encased a layer of water that covered a molten core. As denser interior mass cooled and hardened and penetrated the surface of the water over untold thousands or millions or billions of years, life emerged. The bubble operated like a terrarium on a living room table. It was self-sustaining, "A mist rose up to water the plants." The icy firmament maintained a stable uniformity on the surface of the spinning globe.

Plants and animals replicated and grew in accordance with a mysterious code implanted in every life form at its inception. Science dictates that plants carry this code in their xylem and phloem, animals in their veins and arteries. Even simple singled-celled life forms exhibit it in fluid encased in a membrane. Leviticus 17:11 declares, "The life of every flesh is in the blood." Derived from the original Hebrew, that's an apt modern medical description for the genetic code in every living species.

But how could an ancient Hebrew writer know that? And where did our moral conscience come from? The Bible indicates that originally all plants were edible and every animal was vegetarian. Such a self-perpetuating environment precluded death aside from disease. There is no mention of contamination or disease.

Regardless of a literal interpretation of the Adam and Eve epoch, reasonable people agree on several points. Archeological and biological discoveries all point to northeastern Africa and the southern part of the Middle East, west of the Euphrates River that modern geologists, geographers, and anthropologists call the Fertile Crescent or cradle of civilization. The Bible describes the area as the Garden of Eden, irrigated by the Euphrates, the Pison, the Gihon, and the Hiddekel Rivers.

The Bible says God "put man in the garden to dress it and keep it." That could be interpreted a number of ways, but the basic premise is beyond dispute. The framing of the story supports the notion that morality and intellect were suddenly interjected as civilization emerged, without dashing the hope of finding another Java man or Australopithecine skeleton that predates modern humans. The recent discovery of homo-naledi skeletons in a cave in northern Africa doesn't disrupt the Bible.

Unlike many Christians, Torah literate Jewish physicists and biologists I've had discussions with do not argue that the entire world began 6,000 years ago as the Jewish calendar suggests, or that humanoid type forms were not around prior to that. However, they firmly subscribe to the notion that God implanted his creative will in man around 5,778 years ago as the Bible's genealogical account indicates. The text expands to say people were free to eat fruit from any tree except the one that was the ultimate source of good and evil. Man does not determine good and evil. God does.

That mankind was the pinnacle of God's creation is borne out by the statement that God put people in charge of his garden and delineated the terms of their stewardship. Only an overseer can assign a name to something. God designated Adam and Eve and allowed them to name everything else. Man alone among life forms possessed the creative intelligence to make a wheel, call it a wheel, and relate his discovery to peers who might coordinate their efforts to improve it. God entrusted people with material existence, physical life, animated intelligence, moral conscience, and ultimately free-will to govern themselves and everything around them.

God made the universe. God made Earth. God made plants and animals. And God, however we see him, made mankind to oversee everything He created. The second chapter of Genesis concludes with an observation that the man and woman were naked and unashamed. Physically, mentally, emotionally and spiritually, these perfect specimens were at first open, innocent, naïve, and vulnerable.

3

The First Sin

Scientific research and analysis has yielded many models of our prehistoric past, but none for our actual appearing. Mankind's origin and early development can't be captured for analysis, and cannot be reproduced. No one's view on the matter of how we got here can conclusively be deemed right or wrong. Man's physical nature isn't the object of the Biblical narrative. Those who engage in debates pitting evolution against Biblical creationism are generally misguided. The Bible spends all of two chapters laying the scientific groundwork for man's experience on Earth. The next 1,187 chapters deal with mankind's physical history on a spiritual quest.

Einstein's theory of general relativity and Darwin's theory of evolution are mainstays in modern scientific thinking. Most non-academics are not aware Einstein insisted quantum theory would not reconcile with his work in relativity, and that Darwin used evolution as a template for backtracking to the origins of species. Both offered viable original theorems, though neither has attained the stature of scientific law. Both men in their own lifetimes conceded their extended hypotheses were flawed.

The Bible progresses from physical science to moral philosophy in the third chapter. The famous portrayal of Adam and Eve being tempted in a garden paradise can and should be taken at face value. If a demon magically spoke through a snake and lured a woman into biting an apple, an allegorical serpent slithered into her psyche and tempted her to violate her conscience, or a truth that lies between the contentious extremes, a being that was once calibrated to the will of its creative source severed that bond and sought self-gratification apart from God's design and purpose.

What Eve saw could not be erased. What she did could not be undone. Defiance and immorality were awakened and could not be lulled back to sleep or ignored. Life as it had been, was over. Intelligent beings with moral awareness hungered to know and experience what was forbidden, and chose to violate their conscience. That remains the norm in virtually every culture on Earth. Purity and health contribute to sustaining life, but contamination, compromise, and disease lead to degeneration and death. It could be said that death infiltrated the Earth through man's imprudent appropriation of right and wrong; the knowledge and application of good and evil.

The voice of God came to the man in the garden asking, "Where are you?" Man could not physically hide in the garden God made for him, but he tried to cover his thoughts and shield himself from a probing God. He chose to evade and blame when he could have confessed and sought restoration. For that, he was banished. The premise of the entire Bible is that truth must ultimately prevail, despite the contrary logic of man.

No one can fathom the deep significance of a proverbial tree of life or tree of knowledge apart from the clear understanding that the fruit of our choices mirrors the consequences in our lives no matter what particular environment we are born into. Sin introduced guilt and shame. It always does. Moral compromise led to a scarred and calloused disposition in a deteriorating state that only ends in death.

Had whatever element that sustained life in the Garden of Eden been made available to man in his state of sinful rebellion the perpetuation of life would have been more cruel and dangerous than the natural course that leads to our release with the hope of eventual restoration. Life is a gift. So is death.

People can ingest and assimilate with differing impacts and outcomes. Holy scriptures often contain deeper meanings. Sometimes statements can illuminate truths that are difficult to convey in few words. For those to whom the Bible is sacred, it cannot be mastered. It must be submitted to. Debating the accuracy of Bible interpreters' word choices is left to those who refuse to be mastered and to those who want a different master than the Bible presents. For nonsubscribers, the Bible is open for critique and analysis. For faithful adherents, the Bible feeds the mind and develops a mindset. Truth can be pursued or avoided. But once it is confronted, it must be accepted, ignored or rejected individually.

Staunch religious traditionalists may have already been offended because what has been presented thus far questions ultra-conservative orthodoxy. Secular humanists might put this book aside because it holds the prospect of supporting a source of accountability beyond our conventional realm of measurement and understanding. But those who haven't closed their minds to the prospect of truth beyond their prior discovery will enjoy probing these pages. Unfortunately, we must trudge before we can soar.

The third chapter of Genesis establishes several principles that guide the Bible's story. First, it defines God and man and establishes their ongoing relationship. Second, it defines righteousness and sin and describes the agencies, paths, and ends of each. Third, it sets the stage for a blessed hope for mankind that has been passed down through a species, a race, a nation, a family, and ultimately a single man. It also establishes the relevant foundation of various rituals and ceremonies that reflect an understanding and commitment to the ongoing purpose of God in man.

Sin compelled God to sacrifice the lives of animals he created in order to cloak or cover those he entrusted to steward his garden paradise. That introduced death into a garden of life. Homo-sapiens alone among all current and prehistoric primates display an early inclination to bathe and defecate in private. The awareness, or even shame, of nakedness emerges without stimulation or encouragement as a desire to cover delicate anatomical parts with clothing as we mature into self-awareness. Nudists grow into a comfort with nakedness, unlike every other species. Perverts obsess over it.

The third chapter of Genesis sets the stage for all the historical, legal, and prophetic utterances to follow in the subsequent 1,186 chapters penned by at least 40 different authors over a period of about 1,600 years. The synergy and accuracy of the separate accounts submitted by so many people over such a long period of time is beyond incredible. In its totality the Bible lays out a simple, complete, and unambiguous depiction of spiritual life in a material world from beginning to glorious end. Were the Bible not a blueprint for man's purpose and existence, how else could one explain how closely life on Earth follows the outline of its pages?

4

The First Crime

Adam and Eve gave birth to Cain and Abel. Contrary to the cursory observation of a large number of Bible novices, and even a good number of Bible thumpers, the word "only" does not appear in the original text. The Bible does not state that people began to proliferate because the original pair had two boys. It does say they had another son later. But that's all it specifically says about Adam and Eve and their original family. The Bible identifies those who are essential to its stories and who matter in the broad spectrum of man's history. Each of the particular souls listed by name in the early annals of the Bible affected your present. What you glean from them affects your future.

Cain and Abel lived off the land. They cultivated fields and raised animals. They were aware of their parents' failings, and the Bible suggests they made routine ritualistic offerings to appease the God their parents sought to introduce to them. Cain brought crops from his field, and Abel offered lambs from his flock. The Bible indicates the young men both realized that God was pleased with Abel's sacrifice, but didn't have much regard for what Cain submitted. Cain envied Abel's accolade.

Evidently, a "blood sacrifice" was expected from the inception of worship. The life of God's animals had been taken to make coverings for people's sin in the garden. A proper offering would entail the sacrifice of a domesticated animal on the altar of remembrance. If life is contained and coded in the blood of every creature as the Bible states and science has confirmed, blood would somehow hold the key to redemption from the onset.

Those who focus on offering an object like grain or money have a materialistic mindset. True spiritual worship has always required the very real and permanent sacrifice of that which cannot be measured, replaced, or reinstated. The God of the Bible has forever demanded life to be sacrificed. True sacrifice can be painful, and it is always inconvenient. The degree to which a servant's worship becomes an imposition in his life, more often than not, indicates willfulness and a declining level of commitment.

Instead of heeding the nagging of his spirit to simply do what God was urging him to do in the way God was inspiring him to do it, Cain rebelled. Unlike Eve, who was enticed, or Adam who conformed, Cain plotted how he might appease his insolent spirit. In a jealous rage Cain lured his brother to his field and slayed him. Clearly, he did not bring a grain offering because he was averse to or squeamish about spilling blood as some have taught. Cain was simply willful and self-accommodating; in a word, sinful.

The intimate transmission governed by the curious coded fluid God injects into every unique living creature at its inception cried to God when it spilled into the ground. The signal God planted in Abel's blood spiked then turned to static before going silent like a dying radio. Cain's sensors were spiking too, but he had grown indifferent. Interference blocked his conscience as God tried to communicate with him the way God confronted his father in the garden. Instead of confessing and showing remorse, Cain evaded God and advanced his moral decay, for which he too was banished.

If each man is a steward upon God's Earth it is not for him to seize another's life or even commandeer his own. Cain corrupted God's natural prescribed order severing the cord of life. A rosebud clipped from its vine still blooms and appears living and vibrant, yet from the time it is severed every physical fiber is doomed. Without a provision to reestablish the link that was damaged Cain too would be lost.

Without means to recalibrate, Cain was destined to exist at enmity with God and man. He lived the rest of his days in anxiety, indifferent to God and out of tune with nature. The Bible declares that Cain settled in the land of Nod, east of Eden. He took two wives and had many sons. He established and named the first city after his son Enoch while Adam and Seth still sojourned in forests and fertile valleys.

The Lamech dynasty, attributed to Cain's great great grandson has been unearthed, and artifacts from his era are presently on display. Prior to recent archeological discoveries, it was believed brass and iron did not exist as formed instruments until late in man's history. The Bible indicates that men of Lamech's era mastered the use of copper and iron and enjoyed musical instruments. They built cities of brick and stone and prospered in agriculture, ranching, and various modes of commerce.

Notwithstanding numerous skeletal finds that proved to be scientific scams or clearly not-quite-human early humanoid cave dwellers, archeological discoveries have consistently confirmed that civilizations of genuine humans appeared suddenly upon the Earth. The earliest distinguishable homo-sapiens may actually have been physically and intellectually superior to modern men, yet without the means and resources that make people appear advanced today.

Modern anthropology now tells us that the original Xia dynasty in China developed 5,000 years ago rather than 8,000 as previously thought. The earliest record speaks of "the great stream flowing north to form nine rivers that empty into the sea." That describes the Nile River perfectly, but hardly draws illusions of the famous Yellow River that flows east to west with no branching deltas. Archeologists are now looking into a recently uncovered Middle Eastern Hyksos connection to confirm the unknown origin of the Chinese race. Myths of supernatural Chinese origin have been closely guarded and perpetuated for centuries by tyrants with a vested interest.

Human beings truly are distinct among God's creatures. Man hasn't changed much. We are still willful creative beings with a unique moral conscience. Individuals are unique but humanity is universal and timeless. Like the branching Nile River delta, men's obvious physical distinctions diverge over time and cannot be fused. But, like tributaries of the Yellow River, our mutual moral awareness points us to a singular compass point. A line from west to east superimposed over a line south to north unveils a symbol that may hold the key to man's source and destiny.

5

Adam's Early Descendants

After Cain slew Abel, Adam and Eve had another son and named him Seth. Seth had a son named Enos. The Bible says that in the third generation, "People began to call upon the name of the Lord." That can be interpreted from the original Hebrew to indicate people searched for an overseer they only knew secondhand. Successive generations drifted yet further and their relationship with God became ever more distant as men became more self-oriented and independent.

These are the first ten generations from Adam according to the fifth chapter of Genesis:

Name	Word Meaning	Year Born	Age at Son's Birth	Years Lived	Year Died
Adam	Man	0	130	930	930
Seth	Appointed	130	105	912	1042
Enosh	Mortal	235	90	905	1140
Kenan	Sorrow	325	70	910	1235
Mahalel	Bless God	395	65	895	1290
Jared	Descend	460	162	962	1422
Enoch	Instruct	622	65	365	987*
Methuselah	Death brings*	687	187	969	1656*
Lamech	Despairing	874	182	777	1651
Noah	Comfort	1056	502	950	2006

Adam first had Cain and Abel. Cain killed his brother and his own lineage was lost in a cataclysmic flood event. The Bible says Enoch communed closely with God and at the age of 365, "God took him". The text does not express that Enoch ever strayed from God or ever died. Lamech was 182 when he had Noah and lived to be 777, dying five years before the great flood. Noah was 600 years old at the time of the flood so he was born 1,056 years after Adam was created and there are 1,656 years of recorded genealogy from the introduction of Adam to the flood that wiped out Noah's kindred in the land.

The Bible does not state that those mentioned above were firstborn sons of their fathers, though some hold that tradition. Nor does it reference the hundreds of other offspring that came from each one over such a long lifespan when men were commissioned to reproduce and subdue the Earth. The genealogy given simply verifies the specific male lineage from Adam to Noah over ten generations. Hundreds of thousands of names were lost in the great flood, so at this point they are irrelevant.

Pre-flood lifespans were ten times longer than in modern times. That may have to do with conditions on Earth prior to the flood, especially if there was a layer of ice or heavy mist that encased the globe and provided a different environment than we are accustomed to. Ultraviolet sun rays would have been filtered out. Air would have been oxygen rich and food sources abundant and nutritious. At its inception Earth is described as a garden paradise meant to sustain life. The original Hebrew text depicts an enclosed park. Hyperbaric chambers are now commonly utilized to heal, sustain, enhance and even extend human life. The ancient Greek word paradeisos is properly translated "enclosed garden".

The creation story was passed down orally from those who were intimately familiar with it. Each patriarch listed overlapped several generations. Noah would have known his lineage and passed it down to his children's children after the flood for later recording. Methuselah's life overlapped Adam's by 243 years and Methuselah died 502 years after Noah was born. Noah's sons were his great grandchildren.

Other ancient civilizations had traditions of extreme longevity prior to a great flood event. Notably, there were ten Babylonian kingdoms that parallel the Biblical pre-flood descendants of Adam, though the names are different. None of those listings is known to precede the Biblical account, though some might argue the point. It makes no difference of consequence.

The Bible states that successive generations drifted from the God of their fathers, "but Enoch walked with God, and he was not, for God took him." Literal translation reveals that Enoch had a communal relationship with God and at the age of 365 God snatched him from Earth. He is the first person in the Bible for whom there is no record of death, and curiously, no indication of sin. The Bible specifies Enoch's allegiance to God never waned. Many Christian theologians propose this rapture of the faithful prior to a dreadful world event is a preview of another Biblical occurrence forecasted at the end of time.

Several pre-flood era cities mentioned in the Bible have been excavated. We know from archeological finds at Ur, Erech, Eridu, Kish, Obeid, Sippar, and many other sites, that these cities held public and private buildings, family dwellings, and common grounds. They employed the use of stone and metal implements, clay bricks baked in ovens, and even copper mirrors. Painted plaster adorned some walls, pottery was abundant, and civilizations were surprisingly advanced. Tablets alluding to laws, kings, and transactions were found in what appeared to be libraries. Men who lived in the Ante-Diluvian period were both highly intellectual and very materialistic.

Among abundant oddities in the pre-flood Biblical narrative that beckon study and analysis, some stand out. First, the Hebrew expression for God used in Genesis 1:1, Elohim, is in the plural form. Just as we might say, a thing, a couple of things, or some things, the Hebrews delineated between one object, two, and three or more. Elohim refers to a single entity consisting of at least three distinct components.

Second, the Hebrew term *adam* is the generic English term for *man*, and adamah is mud. Eve means something akin to mother of life, understood as the source of other men (boys and girls). Even the names of the ten patriarchs from Adam to Noah provide a daunting correlation when listed by their translation to English. "Adam seth enosh kenan mahalel jared enoch methuselah lamech noah," becomes, "Man appointed mortal sorrow blessed descend teaching inheritance despairing comfort." The ten terms, or names, may align with the attributes of a coming savior.

The translation of terms listed above is open to debate, but the record allows for such mystical interpretations that often become fodder for questioning what is not specifically stated. This illustrates how people who argue for or against the Bible stray when they go beyond what the text clearly conveys in literal terms. Apart from taking words out of context or misrepresenting their meaning, there is no problem reconciling the Biblical record with known science and history. Regardless of a person's view of the stories, there is something different and special about the Holy Bible in all of its forms and iterations that warrants attention and respect.

6

A Great Flood

Using a base of approximately 4000 BC as the time Middle Eastern civilizations sprang up along the Euphrates River basin places the colossal flood of Genesis at about 2400 BC according to Biblical genealogical records. The Bible doesn't give exact dates, but constructs a framework that can be confirmed by archeological analysis. There is ample information to place key events.

Like the creation of Earth and proliferation of mankind, many non-Hebrew cultures paid homage to an epoch universal flood in their ancient literature and artifacts. Fossils of fish discovered in mountains and cliffs hundreds of feet above sea level strongly support flood claims. The Hebrews alone recorded years and genealogies that consistently linked the created being with his creator. The Bible text at this point is primarily developing a background for the moral and spiritual underpinnings which are the cornerstone of the book. Nine chapters is less than one tenth of one percent of the entire manuscript. In contrast, major sections of the world's libraries and museums are dedicated to events of the same period.

Noah was a tenth generation offspring of Adam. Adam died only 126 years before Noah was born. Among his ancestors, only Adam, Seth, and Enoch would not have known their prominent descendant. Noah had the potential opportunity to converse with six of his nine forefathers, as well as thousands of uncles and aunts over several generations. Clearly, he ingested their stories and was singularly lauded for his commitment to the God of his fathers.

Cain settled to the east in near proximity to the land where Adam raised Seth. From the record, Seth's descendants gravitated toward godliness and Cain's people became quite worldly. One clan is referred to as sons of God and the other as sons of men. The Bible states the sons of God were attracted to the beautiful and alluring daughters of the sons of men. They intermarried, had children, and compromised themselves; the godly with the ungodly. A race called Nephilim grew larger, stronger, and increasingly more sophisticated than their godly contemporaries. Terribly corrupt and wicked Nephilim, from the Hebrew root nephal that means tyrant, rose to be the most celebrated governors, athletes and merchants among them. Like today, they were their culture's giants in every earthly sense.

The Bible declares that God "looked down" and saw that man's selfish depravity had perverted and corrupted the Earth and disrupted its delicate moral and ecological balance. God was "grieved" that man proved to be such a poor partner in the stewarding of his paradise. God directed Noah to build a huge floating vessel and provided detailed instruction for its construction and use.

At that time an icy firmament still encased and protected the garden planet. It had never rained, but a mist rose up and watered the earth. Men, particularly those described as the sons of God, were assumedly vegetarians. Where God once enjoyed intimacy with his creation, men had become materialistic and aggressive to the point of unceasing violence, ethical transgression, and common sexual perversion and abuse. They no longer saw themselves as stewards of God's paradise, but owner-occupants of a fertile planet to be exploited for their pleasure according to their willful lusts and desires.

When Noah was 500 years old God conveyed that he was about to erase what he initially created and start over with Noah's righteous family. Soon afterward, Noah fathered Shem, Ham and Japheth. The prospect he may have had other sons and daughters is unspecified. The Bible records the names of those central to its story. These four with their wives alone were viewed as righteous among the inhabitants of Earth who had turned away from God. People mocked as Noah spent the next hundred years designing and building a rudderless wooden box that was 450 feet long, 75 feet wide, and 45 feet high. It had three decks, several interior compartments, and a window course above the upper deck.

Over several decades Noah collected pairs of every species of beast that he would ultimately house in the ark. Anthropologists have calculated that there would have been room for 7,000 species of animals inside the vessel. They may have been mature or very young. Food supplies would also have been stored. According to Babylonian custom, Noah may well have been a city king. If so, he would have employed dozens, or even hundreds, of people to construct the ark and gather the animals that eventually made the voyage to safety. Noah might have gathered the first public zoo collection, from which he could have selected pairs from among tame captured stock when it came time to board.

When Noah was 600 years old God ordered him into the ark with his wife, three of his sons and their wives, and the only cargo they would have access to for the next 372 days. The Bible says the door was shut and sealed behind them. It is likely that those whom Noah employed and those who looked on still mocked him until it began to rain seven days later.

A steady deluge persisted for forty days and forty nights while the suspended ice and mist poured from the firmament above onto the surface below. It is impossible to know the population that existed prior to the great flood, but it's reasonable to assume such a first rain that purged the atmosphere of a known abundance of water vapor could easily have wiped out ten generations of inhabitants that settled along the rivers of the region.

Their vessel floated for 150 days as the water slowly and calmly receded. It rested on Mount Ararat in Armenia at an altitude of 16,000 feet, approximately 500 miles from where it most likely started. At the foot of the mountain lies the ancient city of Nakhichevan, which means, "Here Noah settled." Ancient rock carvings found in the last century depict animals like alligators that are clearly not native to the area.

Expeditions over several centuries have hinted at the ark's discovery. Many early explorers claimed to have found it. Modern satellite instruments track what are believed to be its remnants, thought to be captured in a huge mountain glacier. Further breakage and deterioration will occur for as long as the Turkish government continues to prohibit exploration on Mount Ararat.

7

Tower of Babel

New developments enable us to track our human ancestry from DNA samples. It appears from our most recent scientific evidence that all branches of hominids probably originated around northeast Africa at the southwest extreme of the previously calculated Biblical cradle of civilization. This suggests the Hebrew notion of a divine encounter that sanctioned mankind about six thousand years ago is more viable than skeptics previously believed. With carbon dating in dispute over the half-life of the carbon 14 isotope only the timing is now questioned.

After the great flood the icy firmament that encased and shielded the garden planet was gone. The sky was different when Noah came out of the ark. At the sight of what would have been the first rainbow ever seen, Noah came to understand there would never be another such flood to purge the Earth again. He released the animals from the ark to repopulate an altered terrain whose climate was forever changed and now less stable. Noah offered some of the animals he carried to God on an altar, and the diet of both men and beasts became notably carnivorous.

Noah's family settled peacefully and began to farm the land in the valley at the foot of Mount Ararat. Over time, they migrated along the Euphrates back toward the land of their origin. Noah's sons were Shem, Japheth, and Ham. And Ham had a son named Canaan. The story of God's engagement with men on Earth was now reconsolidated in the family of Noah.

Noah indulged in wine he fermented from an early crop. He danced naked in his tent until he passed out or fell asleep. His son, Ham, discovered him and mockingly divulged what he saw with his brothers, who respectfully covered their father without looking upon him in his exposed and vulnerable condition. When Noah came to and realized what had happened, he was furious that Ham would make a public spectacle of his private folly. He cursed Ham and prophesied all the descendants of Ham's son Canaan would assume a servile role.

That prediction was borne out in recorded history, and is still the object of strife between contentious distant cousins. Early in the restart, the Bible made a strong statement that every man's actions are observed by God individually, and no man can publicly expose another man's sin without invoking repercussion upon his own house. Sin is always personal and supremely serious.

The next major episode of the Bible confirms that men remained naturally ambitious and persistently willful, even after the flood. Noah's great grandson, Nimrod, was called a mighty man of Earth. He was a grandson of Ham by his son Cush and thus a nephew of Canaan. An ancient Babylonian representation of a king defending his people from an attacking mountain lion is said to represent the great king Nimrod who founded the city of Babylon.

Nimrod established a government that oversaw several large cities over a three hundred mile radius. He appears to have been the first imperialist ruler. Archeology has conclusively confirmed the once questioned historical accuracy of tenth chapter of Genesis. Cuneiform inscriptions tell that Nineveh was established by Assur and colonized from Babylon by Merodach, which turned out to be another name for Nimrod. Thus arose the Assyrians and Babylonians.

Excavation of ziggurats in these major cities lends credence and understanding to the story of a towering structure in a city called Babel. A ziggurat could be described as an infant version of an apartment building, a mall, a skyscraper, and pyramid in a single structure. Each layer could have housed an independent clan or community. Ziggurats were an ingenious development. Some are believed to have towered 120 feet with shrines and altars on a flat roof. Ziggurats made a strong statement. Men were no longer content to be a race of stewards, but determined to dominate their world and govern themselves.

Several generations of Shem, Ham and Japheth's descendants are listed in the tenth chapter of Genesis. They lived together as communal families for many years. They shared a single culture and language. That changed as they multiplied and spread. Diverse interests and rival spirits drew them apart. Some even introduced strange new gods, or turned away from worshipping any god at all. Family groups no longer cooperated. They no longer communicated.

Over subsequent generations the Bible asserts that the people of Japheth moved north and became the inhabitants of Europe and northern Asia, usually associated with Caucasian races. The people of Ham predominantly went south to occupy the African continent. The people of Shem stayed in the region and moved eastward. Semites compose most of the tribes and nation-states that are the focus of almost all of the major early encounters in the Bible.

According to the Bible, Noah lived 350 years after the flood. From that point, man's longevity steadily declined to about 120 years for a normal person. Shem was born 98 years before the flood and lived to be 600. His son Arpachshad died at 438, his grandson Shelah 433, and his great-grandson Eber 464. Eber's son Peleg lived to the age of 239, as did Peleg's son Reu. Reu's son Serug died at 230. Serug's son Nahor lived to be only 148, and his son Terah lived until he was

205. Thereafter, recorded mortality does not exceed 200 years again.

Recorded biblical genealogy from Adam to the birth of Noah adds up to 1,056 years in ten generations. The period from Noah's birth to the birth of Abram ten generations later yields 956 years. King David would be born roughly a thousand years later, and Jesus of Nazareth would arrive a thousand years after that. It has been approximately two thousand years since Jesus walked among men. Six one-thousand year increments assume special significance in relation to the seven day creation epoch and biblical eschatology that projects a final thousand year phase of peace and rest on Earth after six millenniums of human domination because the Bible declares, "a day is as a thousand years and a thousand years is but a day to God."

Part 2

Hebraic Foundation

8

Call of Abraham

After the flood, most families that descended from Ham moved south, but one large clan settled along the Mediterranean Sea before they reached the African continent. Much of the land they occupied that bore the name of their great ancestor Canaan became what we know as Israel and Palestine, and has endured continual siege and conquest over many centuries. This is the area most closely associated with the characters and events of the Bible.

Egypt, to the south, was first called Mizraim according to secular archeology. Mizraim was the eldest of Ham's four sons listed in the Bible. Thirty-one documented Egyptian dynasties ruled from the time of Mizraim to the close of the Old Testament portion of the Bible. The rest of Ham's sons became the tribes and nation-states of Africa. People who descended from Cush occupied areas we know as Ethiopia and Sudan. Phut's descendants inhabited Libya and regions north and west on the African continent.

Families of Shem remained in their vicinity of origin. One clan of Semites traveled west and dwelt among nomadic tribes who continually raided and pilfered each other. The ancient city king Malachi Zadok established Uru Shalom, which meant city of ultimate peace, in the midst of the clan of Jebus, the third son of Canaan. It is the only permanent settlement in the region to be unearthed from this early period.

Malachi Zadok is transcribed Melchizedek, but the name Melchi, derived from melech that means king, is usually written as Malachi. The name can mean "righteous king" or "just messenger". The word origin, like most Hebrew terms and names, is hard to know because early written Hebrew did not employ vowels. Adoni Zadok, meaning lord of justice, eventually conveyed his kingdom on the same mountain to Joshua after the exodus from Egypt. Some Jewish scholars believe Melchizedek the Semite was sent ahead to establish Jerusalem, and Abraham's tithe of ten percent from the spoils of a conquest was an earnest money deposit. Mixed race Semitic-Jebusite relatives occupied the mountain fortress of Zion until David arrived and secured the note, making Jerusalem the permanent Jewish capital of Earth.

Nine generations from Noah, a Semite named Terah lived among the Chaldeans in the city of Ur. As with Melchizedek, the terms are informative. Ur meant city, and Chaldean depicted people beyond the river. The location and race were understood to be Babylonian. In modern vernacular one might say, "Terah's family took up residence among those of the other side." That would be a colorful biblical statement.

Terah moved from Ur, in what we call Iraq, back to Haran in his homeland of Padan-Aram in a region we know as northern Syria along the Turkish border. Terah had three sons; Haran, Abram, and Nahor, and Haran had a son named Lot. Upon Haran's untimely death in Ur, Abram and his wife Sarai adopted Lot, which was the Semite custom of the day. The family likely had close family ties to Haran. Afterall, Terah lived little more than a hundred miles away and named one of his sons after the patriarch of Haran. Notably, Terah's family was of a class that provided a slave-girl or handmaiden to a young bride like Sarai. When Terah died, Abram became the head of their clan.

In the twelfth chapter of Genesis Abram sensed God calling him to leave his family, friends, and all he knew and depended on, to go to an unfamiliar territory where he would ultimately prosper and thrive. Abram, which meant father of much, took on a new identity. His new name, Abraham, meant father of many. His wife Sarai, meaning princess, became known as Sarah, a chieftain or governess.

Abraham's brother Nahor married Milcah, daughter of the then tribal leader of Haran. Upon Abraham's departure, Nahor assumed the role of clan leader and became prominent there. That would become important later when Abraham and his successive descendants sent their sons home to find suitable brides from their own stock. Abraham's future promise lay in the land of Canaan.

Abraham wasn't accepted among the nomadic Hamites in the largely unsettled territory of Canaan. In fact, he was continually threatened, bullied, and robbed of what he acquired. A famine drove him to seek refuge further south in Egyptian territory, perhaps Sinai or the Negev. While there, he prospered when a pharaoh of Egypt, a descendant of Ham, became infatuated with the beautiful olive skinned Sarah, a descendant of Shem. Pharaoh means king. We think of a pharaoh as a national leader, but originally several pharaohs ruled their cities or regions simultaneously. Abraham sold his bride off as his sister to become one of a particular pharaoh's many wives in order to avoid confrontation.

Abraham proved to be a man of questionable moral strength and integrity, yet he repeatedly enjoyed the protection and blessings of God. On the surface Abraham might appear to have been a scoundrel. Yet, he was a man with an undeniable yearning for his creator. In the midst of character trials his moral conscience was continually drawn back to God. Therein lies the source of his providential blessing. Abraham was not simply a man through whom God chose to pass material blessings. More especially, Abraham was the pioneer of a faith that ensures safe passage beyond a physical earthly pilgrimage. The Bible does not sugarcoat the truth that even the most devout among us are fallible.

What Abraham did warranted his death at the hand of Pharaoh. His treatment of Sarah endangered her and subjected her to ultimate humiliation. Conspicuous greed and dishonesty shattered his reputation among Egyptian society. When he was compelled to leave, he took his wife and the ill-gotten bounty he gained at the hands of good people he took advantage of and returned to Canaan. He had great herds and belongings and continued to prosper to the point that he and his nephew, Lot, began to bicker.

Abraham and Sarah had no children and Lot was in line to receive an inheritance as their adopted son. They agreed to part ways and Abraham gave Lot half of the herd. Abraham settled in the area now commonly known as the West Bank in Israel and Lot chose a picturesque valley to the south. Abraham lived in the shadow of Uru Shalom, the thriving Semite colony governed by the great priest-king Melchizedek. Lot chose the fertile valley descending into the urban Canaanite metropolises of Sodom and Gomorah along the shores of the Dead Sea which boasts the densest concentration of mineral salts of any body of water on Earth, including the oceans. Minerals flow freely into the lowest lake on the planet and are never released because they have no place to go when the water evaporates. The suspended minerals that saturate the lake are worth billions of dollars and it abounds with medicinal properties, yet nothing can live in it. The Bible's lesson is clear.

9

Ishmael & Isaac

Abraham prayed for an heir according to the promise that lured him from Haran to Canaan. On several occasions throughout Genesis God affirmed that Abraham would be blessed with children more numerous than the stars in the sky or the grains of sand on the beach. Wandering through a land he was providentially led to, Abraham sensed God telling him, "Look to the north, south, east and west, as far as you can see. This is the land I have set aside for your descendants."

With Lot removed from his lineage, Abraham needed an heir, but Sarah was barren and both Abraham and Sarah felt time was running out. Abraham was 76 and Sarah was 66 when Sarah reasoned that any child born to her slave, who was legally her property, would ultimately belong to her. Sarah urged Abraham to have a baby with her Egyptian servant, Hagar, and Sarah would consider the child her own.

When Hagar became pregnant with Ishmael a rift naturally developed between Sarah and her longtime handmaid and best friend. Hagar grew jealous of Sarah's marriage to Abraham, and Sarah resented that Hagar had been able to produce a son for him. Sarah was 79 years old when she miraculously got pregnant for the first and only time thirteen years later. The Bible clearly states Sarah was post-menopausal, "It ceased to be with Sarah after the manner of women."

It appears from multiple passages in the Bible that God predetermined to bless Abraham and Sarah with an heir, a baby of their own, only after it was humanly impossible. The miraculous event is a hallmark of the Jewish claim of being favored, or chosen, by God. It also foreshadowed the miraculous incarnation of a future messiah. Those who believed they descended from Sarah, a woman with no capacity to bear children, could reasonably accept the advent of a messiah through a healthy woman who was supernaturally fertilized. Without Isaac there would be no Jews, and hence, no Jesus Christ.

The way it came to be also set the stage for centuries of contention between Abraham's potential heirs. Physical events portended God's plan for the ages. Lot was Abraham's adopted son. As legal heir, Lot was put out of Abraham's will when the two parted company and Abraham paid him half his current wealth. Adversity ultimately arose due to Lot becoming the incestuous forefather of the Moabites and Ammonites with whom the Israelites contended upon their return from captivity hundreds of years later. Neighboring descendants of Abraham are still at odds over land they mutually occupy today.

Ishmael, though Abraham's seed out of wedlock, was legally Sarah's slave property, and thus hers to dispose of according to the custom of their day. Ishmael was legally cut out of Abraham's estate when he was cruelly banished into the wilderness with his mother at Sarah's behest. Abraham asked God to bless Ishmael as he reluctantly sent them away. The pronouncement over what became the tribal nations of Ishmael in the Middle East is unsettling in retrospect. "He will be a wild ass of a man. He will raise his hand against everyone, and everyone's hand will be against him. He will forever be hostile to all his brothers." To this day, true to the blessing prescribed in the Bible, descendants of Ishmael in Arab lands contend with each other and with their Jewish cousins over property and jurisdiction they mutually claim as their inheritance from Abraham.

Wars, treaties, and foreign accords cannot resolve the deep-rooted issues between Semitic Jews and mixed race Arabs. At its core it is not simply a political matter. God assigned a coveted territory we recognize as the state of Israel to Isaac and his offspring, and descendants of his disconsolate half-brother still resent it. This is a perpetual religious conflict allowed by God as an outcropping of human willfulness. According to ancient holy scriptures, Sarah's natural born legitimate son Isaac alone remained in Abraham's household and thus in his will and testament.

Although Abraham loved Isaac, when the favored son came of age God put Abraham to the ultimate test of faith. In a onetime event that illustrated God's purpose for mankind, Abraham clearly heard God directing him to take his now sole heir to Mount Moriah to offer him on an altar in order to prove his devotion to God.

Abraham was bewildered. He would rather have died than take the life of the one he cherished above anything else in the world. Yet, he would not betray the God he followed and dedicated his life to. Abraham was torn and confused, but genuinely trusted God and believed somehow God intended good at the cost of the son in whom he invested his prospective estate and legacy. This illustrated what it actually takes for a person to inherit the predetermined blessed kingdom of God; absolute faith, withholding nothing.

Abraham made his innocent son carry the wood he would be strapped to and burned on up the mountain. Isaac trusted his father unequivocally, so he did not resist. He knew his father intended only the best for him. Isaac had to be old enough and strong enough to carry the wood and Jewish tradition holds that he was 37 years old. Together they set out to please God. Jewish tradition also relays that

Isaac asked to be bound with ropes lest he flinch and be wounded badly rather than killed.

When the time came for Abraham to strike his son with a blade, the Lord stayed his hand. Abraham saw a young ram caught in a nearby thicket and offered the ram instead. God accepted the substitutionary sacrifice and confirmed the blessing that lay in store for future generations. There Isaac modeled the worshipful offering of another innocent son who would willingly lay his life down to fulfill God's demand in that same mountain range two thousand years later.

10

Sodom & Gomorah

Man was intimate with his creator in the garden paradise. He recognized, appreciated, and served the will of the singular multifaceted God that transcends the universe in which we live. When man broke his bond with the unseen force from which he derived physical life, he quite literally altered the course of nature. The Bible is clear and honest about man's moral frailty and does not exempt or excuse its central characters. When any man loses his natural bond with his creative spiritual source in pursuit of his own willful interest or desire, we call that excursion sin.

In a state of sin a man is compelled to lean on his own logic as opposed to the logos, or expressed logic, of his designer. Men make assumptions that bring artificial meaning and order to a complex world of physical, mental and emotional dimensions. When God asks, "Where are you?" or "What have you done?" it's time to reorient and recalibrate back to the original design setting. In a word, repent.

Unrepentant men drift and rationalize. What Satan initially proposed still makes sense to the human psyche. The devil does not lure men to follow him, but to turn from God to direct themselves according to their own logic, ambition, and quest for power, pleasure, or prosperity. Intimacy with and faithful reliance on God is a choice. Paradoxically, when men choose to reject the God of nature and declare moral independence they revert to worshiping futile alternatives and absolving themselves from moral responsibility. Such was the case in Eden. Such was the case in the days of Seth, and Noah, and Abraham. And such is the case today.

Abraham lived in an era when men had lost their primeval knowledge of God and groped in darkness for answers to the mysteries of existence.

We know from archeological finds dating back to his time that the people of Ur, where Abraham grew up, worshiped the rain, sun, fire, and local rivers. Assur, the founder of Assyria, became the chief god of the Assyrians. Likenesses of Assur and other iconic figures were cast into images to be sold and worshipped on a broad, almost universal scale. The chief god of the Babylonians was Marduk, otherwise known as Nimrod. Nimrod is credited with building the great ziggurat cities of Nineveh, Babylon, and many others. He was an imperialist king who spawned hostile violent religions amidst aggressive materialistic people throughout the Middle East.

Seeking power, possessions, and influence, tribes raided each other, killing and robbing their cousins and rationalizing it in the name of their religions. Nomads banded together to form city states that were routinely seized by more powerful clans. One outstanding anomaly was Urushalom, the walled city presided over by the devout Semite priest-king Melchizedek. Further south lay the great Canaanite cities of Sodom, Gomorrah and Zoar. The sprawling metropolis was home to over a million people.

Lot moved from the valley south of Urushalom to the fertile fields closer to Sodom. As his wealth dwindled, occasioned from droughts, raids and other factors, he sought refuge in the secure modern city with its arenas, shops, theaters, multistory buildings, and public projects. The Bible records that, "The stench of perversion and corruption rose to God's nostrils," as in Noah's time. God determined to eradicate the blatant irreverence that was spreading human decay.

One day, Abraham spotted a small band traveling south from the vicinity of Urushalom, or Salem. Over dinner he discovered they were on their way to Sodom and Gomorrah to confirm the gravity of sin that prevailed there. Bear in mind the state of sin, or separation from God, is what opens men to sins, or activities that are contrary to the will of God. These men, or messengers commissioned by God as the term angels would more accurately be translated, were looking for sin in the singular form. They were confirming a condition, not analyzing the sinful behaviors that are the symptoms and evidence of sin.

Knowing that his nephew, Lot, had taken up residence in Sodom, Abraham intervened. "What if you find 50 righteous souls among the people there? Will my Lord spare the 50 or eradicate the whole population?" The spokesman assured Abraham the entire wicked community would be spared for the sake of 50 righteousness people who believed in and followed the true and living God.

Abraham continued to probe, "How about 40? 30? 20? 10?" Each time the spokesman assured him that God judges sin but would not condemn the habitat of the righteous. It is interesting to note that though some rightly say good people have to suffer because of evil in their midst, it's also true that often the only reason evil communities or nations are spared is because a few righteous folks happen to dwell inconspicuously among them.

Upon close scrutiny, the emissaries of God discovered that aside from Lot and his family, the area was devoid of righteousness. Apparently, Lot had compromised as well because he had no influence over his neighbors, friends and family. Even his own sons-in-law mocked when Lot tried to reason with them about his God and the impending crisis.

Lot was ushered out of the city and preserved similar to how Noah was protected in an ark. With the only righteous humans safely evacuated, God bombarded the still currently geologically active area that included the land of the Sodomites with subterranean phosphorous and sulfur that spewed into the sky and fell like balls of fiery lava, destroying every creature and manmade structure. Only Lot, his wife and two daughters were spared. God warned them to flee to a mountain cave and not look back. Lot's wife directed her gaze on what she left behind and reverted to the natural elements she was composed of. She foolishly cast her fate with the material world she grew attached to and was ultimately obliterated along with it.

Although Lot and his daughters were saved, they soon transgressed again. In order to propagate their race, they engaged in incest. Lot fathered a son by his eldest daughter and became the patriarch of the Moabites. He fathered the Ammonites by his second daughter. The effect of their sinful rationalization came to fruition generations later when Israel warred against their close cousins to regain access to their promised land. Today Israel is compelled to resist other mixed descendants of Canaan, Lot and Ishmael in the same region under the defiant banners of Hamas, Hezbollah, Al Qaeda and the Islamic State.

11

Esau and Jacob

In the course of time, Abraham sent one of his servants to his brother Nahor in Padan-Aram to secure a bride for his son Isaac. Isaac's wife Rebekah gave birth to paternal twins and the boys were very different. Esau was first out of the womb with thick hair and a ruddy complexion. He was already active and strong. The second child was physically beautiful, quiet and alert. Curiously, he grasped his older brother's ankle through the birthing process. They called him Jacob, which meant usurper or one who supplants, because he already seemed to be trying to overtake his brother. Isaac immediately favored Esau, the more physically robust child. Rebekah preferred the clearly pensive more responsive one.

Esau grew up to be a herdsman and a hunter. Jacob preferred administrative and domestic affairs. One day Esau came in famished from working the fields and asked Jacob for a portion of the lamb stew he was making. Esau was lightheaded and exhausted, and he desperately wanted something to eat. Jacob demanded something in return. He bargained for Esau's birthright which assured him of a greater portion of Isaac's estate, and more significantly, oversight of the family. Esau flippantly agreed, ate his bowl of stew, and dismissed it.

Years later, when their father was near death, feeble and blind, the pledge was fulfilled and Jacob truly supplanted his older brother. Isaac sensed he didn't have long upon the Earth, so he told Esau to kill a ram and make some of his favorite stew. Then he would give his son a formal blessing and turn the reins of the family over to him. Rebekah overheard it and sent for Jacob.

Together they plotted that Jacob would immediately make his lamb stew, season it like Esau seasoned his ram stew, put on Esau's clothes to smell like Esau, and put lambskins over his arms to bulk up and feel more like his older brother. While Esau was still hunting, Jacob presented himself to Isaac, fed his father, and received the family blessing. In essence, he tricked his father and cheated his brother.

Esau was furious. Isaac could not legally retract the blessing he gave to Jacob. Instead, he prayed a different blessing over Esau. Esau would be great in the land but never reign over his brother or his brother's descendants. Such is the case in Palestine to this day. Jacob was certain that when their father died Esau would kill him for what he had done.

The birthright was to be honored and preserved. The fact that Esau took a wife from one of the local clans displeased Isaac and Rebekah. Esau found another wife from among his cousins in Ishmael's clan making matters worse. Isaac and Rebekah arranged to send Jacob to Haran to work for his uncle Laban who was Rebekah's older brother and find a suitable bride from among their own untarnished bloodline. Jacob gladly, and quickly, departed for his ancestral home.

On his way to Haran, Jacob fell into a trance and envisioned a ladder springing up from a rock. Angels ascended on one side and descended from the other. One brought a message to Jacob. God decreed that the land around him would one day belong to Jacob and his offspring. Jacob anointed the stone and called his altar Beth

El, or House of God. King Jeroboam of Israel built a sanctuary and placed two golden calves there many generations later. The actual site was rediscovered by archeologist William Albright near the village of Beitin in the 1930s.

In Haran Jacob fell in love with Laban's beautiful daughter, Rachael. He agreed to work seven years for her hand in marriage. At the end of seven years Laban hosted a grand wedding, but the veiled young bride he sent into Jacob's tent was Leah, Rachael's homely older sister. Jacob unwittingly consummated the marriage.

Laban smugly contended that Jacob should have known the universal Semite custom of marrying off the daughters in a family by birth order. If Jacob wanted Rachael, he had to stay and work for Laban seven more years. A deceitful young man fell prey to his equally onerous uncle. Jacob was livid, but there was nothing he could do. Jacob loved Rachael. He agreed to the terms. Jacob married Rachael when his seven day wedding celebration for Leah concluded, but he remained with Laban seven more years.

Leah gave Jacob six sons; Reuben, Simeon, Levi, Judah, Issachar and Zebulon. When Rachel saw that she wasn't having any children, she convinced Jacob to make babies with her handmaid, Bilhah. The servant girl conceived Dan and Naphtali.

Leah also offered her handmaid, and Zilpah bore Jacob Gad and Asher. After ten sons had been born, Rachael at last got pregnant and bore Joseph. Much later she gave birth to Benjamin. From among these twelve sons would come the tribes of Israel and their priests.

Jacob proved himself to be industrious, frugal, and crafty. He rose to become the clan's chief administrator and outwitted Laban to gain claim to most of his livestock. This time the deceptive uncle fell prey to his onerous nephew. Wealthy beyond his expectation, Jacob returned to Canaan.

The Bible says that on the way home Jacob "wrestled with God all night long." Jacob clung to God and would not let go. There God declared that Jacob would be known as Isra El, or "contends with God", depicting the epoch scrap. Jacob struggled to cling to God. Now the nation that descended from Israel would wrestle with its obedience to God for centuries to come.

12

The Emergence of Israel

It had been twenty years since Jacob snatched the family birthright and fled to Haran virtually empty handed. Divine premonitions were lining up and being fulfilled in Abraham, Isaac, and now Jacob. Jacob returned to Canaan with great herds and flocks, servants and possessions, as well as eleven sons by two wives and two concubines, or mistresses.

When Jacob left, Isaac seemed to be waning and Esau had vowed to get revenge. Jacob expected the worst, but was received well by his brother. Jacob also found his father still alive and affectionate toward him. Again, despite his questionable integrity and standing, a patriarch of the Hebrews was undeservedly exonerated of his bad behavior and shown unmerited favor.

Jacob settled in the land of Hamor the Hittite chieftain, bought a parcel of land, and built an altar to God. Leah's daughter, Dinah, made friends with some local girls and went to visit them in their village. Hamor's narcissistic son, Shechem, was overcome with the beautiful stranger and raped her. Then he asked his father to go to her parents and arrange a marriage.

Dinah's brothers were beyond furious, but Jacob welcomed Hamor and Shechem into his tent to hear them out. The Hittites proposed a treaty whereby the Hebrews would intermarry with Hamor's clan and integrate into Canaanite society. They didn't realize that Jacob's family had no intention of diluting or compromising their bloodline.

Shechem begged them to let him marry their sister and pledged that he would pay any price for her. They told him they could not intermarry with an uncircumcised race but proposed that if every male in Hamor's household agreed to be circumcised, they would consider it.

Hamor compelled every man and boy under his influence to be circumcised. Three days after the mass circumcision, the men were so sore they couldn't walk. Two of Dinah's older brothers, Simeon and Levi, went into the village and put their swords to every male, starting with Shechem and Hamor. They plundered the village, rounded up the flocks and herds, and took every female and infant male hostage.

Jacob was beside himself. Certain that every Canaanite cousin of Hamor the Hittite would soon converge on his small clan, Jacob went to Bethel to worship, and then moved on to Hebron, Abraham's old home. As it turned out, the two brothers had struck such fear in every Canaanite that no one dared attack.

The descendants of Ham, along with the sons of Ishmael and Esau who had integrated into their culture, continued to raid each other. However, they didn't provoke the descendants of Shem in Hebron or Urushalom. From that time forward all the neighboring clans reverently referred to their peculiar bold neighbors only as Israel, people who contended with God. Men, women, and children of Israel were safe as long as they stayed within their borders or traveled in groups.

Along the way from Bethel to Hebron, Rachael died in childbirth. Jacob named their son Benjamin, or son of sorrow, and buried his wife in a cave in the wilderness of Ramah. Jacob had a special love for Rachael and showed favor to her sons over all his other children. He even made a colorful coat for Joseph, Rachael's firstborn, so he would stand out among his brothers. When Jacob sent his other sons to work in the fields, he kept Joseph by his side.

Joseph was notably intelligent and very self-confident. He was a dreamer who liked to interpret dreams. On one occasion over a meal he shared a dream in which his brothers bowed to him as though he was their king. On another, he broadcasted that he would be their caretaker. The older half-brothers grew up resenting the spoiled little brat, but the traits that irritated them would one day enable Joseph to save their blossoming nation.

One day Jacob sent Joseph out to the pasture to check on his brothers. When they spotted him, they conspired against him. They determined to kill him and be rid of the menace. Reuben convinced the others to throw Joseph into a well he couldn't escape from. All along, he intended to come back and rescue him. Just then, a caravan of Ishmaelite spice merchants approached on their way to Egypt. Judah suggested that instead of killing their brother they should sell him to the heathens as though he was their slave. Clearly, Joseph's objections weren't credible in the face of his brothers' insistence.

When the brothers considered what they had done and how it would affect their father, they took Joseph's multicolored coat, ripped it, and stained it with the blood of a lamb from their flock. They returned from the field and presented the coat to Jacob claiming to have found it on their way home. They convinced their father that Joseph had been attacked and eaten by a wild beast.

Jacob fell into a fit of grief and depression that lasted for years. He despaired in the belief that he had sent his highly favored son to his death. Meanwhile, Joseph was bound for Egypt, a slave with a haughty attitude who insisted on presenting what must have been perceived as an unbelievable pretense that no one took seriously.

13

Joseph in Egypt

Joseph was taken to an Egyptian slave market and sold to a military commander by the name of Potiphar. Over time, Joseph gained Potiphar's absolute confidence and trust and rose to be the chief administrator over Potiphar's entire household.

Joseph was charismatic and attractive. Potiphar's wife tried to seduce him, but he repeatedly spurned her advances. On one occasion she cornered him when no one else was around. She grabbed his robe and wouldn't let go. He shed his garment and ran away. When Potiphar came home she showed him the robe and claimed Joseph assaulted her. By law and custom Potiphar could have executed Joseph if he believed her. To save face he had Joseph arrested and put in prison.

In prison Joseph met the Pharaoh's royal baker and royal cupbearer, who had somehow offended their master and gotten thrown in jail too. The men both had dreams they shared with Joseph. The cupbearer saw three clusters of grapes. He pressed the grapes into Pharaoh's cup, handed it to him, and he drank. The baker made three cakes he put in a basket where vultures came and pecked at them.

Joseph analyzed their dreams and accurately forecasted that in three days the cupbearer would be restored to his position, but the baker would be put to death. Three days later, the cupbearer was reinstated and the baker was executed. Back in the palace the cupbearer forgot about Joseph until Pharaoh was plagued with troubling recurring dreams. Pharaoh summoned his priests, magicians and wizards, but no one could help him understand the meaning of his dreams. In one instance, seven fat cows were devoured by seven lean ones. In another, seven hardy wholesome stalks of wheat were overtaken by seven stalks that bore no grain.

The cupbearer heard about it and told Pharaoh about the young man in prison who accurately forecasted his dream and that of the baker. Pharaoh sent for Joseph, who shaved and groomed himself suitably to come before the king of Egypt. Once before Pharaoh, Joseph did not advance his own needs and interests, but succinctly analyzed the king's dreams, crediting God with his insights, and made an ingenious recommendation.

Joseph told Pharaoh that both dreams alluded to seven years of coming bounty followed by seven years of drought in the land. Prosperity would abound for seven years, only to be followed by seven years of famine that would devour the gains and ravage the country. Then Joseph advised Pharaoh to look among his ranks and locate the best administrator he could find to oversee the gathering and distribution of food staples for the next fourteen critical years.

Pharaoh was impressed. He appointed Joseph to his cabinet and put him in charge of the project. The Hebrew slave, a son of Israel, became the grand vizier of the land of Egypt, Prime Minister of the commercial capital of the known world. The Bible says Joseph oversaw the building of storage facilities and the collection of excess harvest grain over the next seven years. Egypt flourished when the great famine came, and people from all over the Levant streamed to Egypt to acquire food.

Joseph married the daughter of the priest of On and had two sons.

Though he governed a heathen nation and married into a family of idol worshippers, Joseph was so devout that he privately maintained his childhood faith in the God of Abraham, Isaac, and Jacob, and passed his faith down to his sons.

Joseph's brothers were among those who came to Egypt to buy grain. Looking and speaking like a native Egyptian, Joseph spotted them at a market and engaged them through a translator, so as to not divulge his true identity. Joseph not only filled their caravan with more wheat than they could afford, he stashed their money in their grain-sacks so they obtained it for free. Jacob was pleased until he found the money. The onetime usurper was a changed man and demanded to pay what he owed. He sent his sons back to get more grain and to pay what was rightfully due. Young Benjamin, Joseph's little brother, accompanied them.

This time Joseph disclosed who he was and forgave them, "Don't lament over selling me into slavery. God has sent me here before you that I might save your lives and preserve our posterity." He invited his brothers to bring the entire clan to Egypt where he could ensure their safety through the worsening drought.

Jacob longed to be reunited with Joseph but was reluctant until he was convinced that his descendants would return to occupy their homeland when the drought ended. Seventy-two people who composed the entire household of Israel departed for Egypt, the most advanced civilization of that day, to be spared and nurtured through a trying time.

On his deathbed in Egypt Jacob called his sons to his side to bless them. Before he began, he initiated a formal ceremony wherein he adopted Joseph's sons, Manasseh and Ephraim. This legal gesture allowed Jacob to reinstate his lost son Joseph's family back into his will and to provide a coveted double portion to his favorite son. Levi, Jacob's third eldest, became a nation of priests embedded in the other tribes. That left twelve among whom property, and ultimately territory back home, would eventually be distributed. That's how twelve sons and two grandsons became the twelve Jewish tribal nations.

Each of the blessings Jacob prophesied over his sons materialized in the course of subsequent generations. Most notably, Jacob passed the birthright of the firstborn that included a double portion of his estate and oversight of the family over Reuben because he secretly slept with his father's concubine, or mistress. He also passed it over Simeon and Levi for their violent aggression toward the clan of Hamor. Ultimately he gave it to Judah, the fourth born, from whom would come King David, and ultimately Jesus Christ.

14

Israel in Bondage

S cholars have searched Egyptian records for centuries looking for evidence of Joseph's reign in Egypt. The recent discovery of fragments from a fourteen foot statue that stood in a public square in Avaris, Egypt, is believed by many to be dedicated to Joseph, called Zaphenath-paneah in the Bible. The statue was placed in the basement of a museum in Cairo after it was uncovered by Professor Manfred Bietak in 1986 after forty years of digging at the same site. It has never been put on public display.

It appears that Zaphenath-paneah was not a name but a title for a business administrator. Archeology indicates he was also known as Imhotep. The statue is dedicated to "The Man", Ha Ish in Egyptian and Ish Ivri in Hebrew. Avaris was a community in Goshen where the Hebrews were concentrated. The statue has been dated at around 1700 BC, a couple hundred years before the Exodus. A tomb associated with the statue was found empty. It could have been looted, or it could be confirmation that Joseph's bones were carried back to Canaan as the Bible states.

The people who first settled Egypt were Hamites of Mizraim's lineage. The Hyksos who came later were a blend of Hamites and Semites. Talented Semites like Joseph who integrated into Egyptian society were welcomed into high ranking government roles. Joseph mastered the language and adopted Egyptian dress and customs. He assumed an Egyptian identity and lived among the Egyptian hierarchy. The Hyksos arrived from 1800-1550 BC and introduced the horse drawn chariot that became a staple of Egyptian military warfare and transport. The Bible states that Pharaoh assigned Joseph to "ride in the second chariot."

An ancient 42 column hieroglyph dated several centuries BC was carved into a granite cliff along the Nile River near Aswan, Egypt. It depicts a seven year famine but does not give a date for the famine and because of damage and weathering does not yield significant details needed to confirm or refute the narrative of Genesis.

The seventy-two member clan of Jacob moved to Egypt, settled in the lush region of Goshen and kept to themselves. They intended a temporary sojourn and isolated themselves to maintain their customs and preserve their religion. The drought was not severe in Goshen, and Israel prospered. When the famine passed, the people stayed. They were settled and comfortable, and they grew accustomed to their new surroundings. The climate was good and the commerce was excellent. The nation of interlopers took Jacob back to be buried with his forefathers, but they were in no rush to get back to Canaan.

Time passed and subsequent generations had even less interest in returning. Eventually, a Pharaoh who "did not know Joseph" arose. The new Pharaoh resented that tens of thousands would not integrate into Egyptian society and prospered to the point they posed a potential threat to his kingdom. The entire Hebrew population was subjected to slavery and put in hard bondage as wards of the state.

The people of God became too attached to their material holdings to leave them and return to their roots. At first devoted to God's will, they grew independent, then attached, then entangled, then dependent, then bound. That is a repeated Biblical progression.

When God called Abraham out of Haran to a land that was settled by nomadic warrior tribes, the one safe haven in the region was Uru Shalom. Abraham was beckoned to a land where he met and paid homage to Melchizedek, the priest-king who strayed from the other clans of Shem and settled amidst hostile tribes. Abraham's descendants, clinging to the promises of God through Jacob, were destined to return and reclaim the ancient city, now better known as Jerusalem, as their Semite homeland capitol.

Abraham consistently and emphatically impressed on his children and their subsequent generations that he had a covenant with God, a contract. God would use Abraham to make a great nation that would occupy the land he dwelled in as far as he could see. Specifically the Bible says, "He that cometh forth out of thine own bowels shall be thine heir. I am the Lord thy God that brought thee out of Ur of the Chaldees to give thee this land to inherit it."

On a subsequent occasion Abraham heard God say, "Know of a surety that thy seed shall be a stranger in a land that is not theirs, and shall serve them there. And they shall afflict them four hundred years. And also that nation whom they shall serve, will I judge. And afterward they shall come out with great substance. And thou shalt go to thy fathers in peace. Thou shalt be buried in a good old age."

Abraham had gone to Egypt to avoid an earlier drought. Isaac had a similar experience. Both patriarchs allowed their spirituality to yield to materialism. Had God not insulated them, they were both destined for ruin. Lot found himself trapped in the lucrative but perverse walls of Sodom. He ultimately lost everything he valued, including his family and his posterity.

Material adversity and challenge drives even devout men to seek shelter and refuge. Men are naturally attracted to physical comfort, convenience and prosperity. When a man looks to his provision and loses sight of his provider he becomes vulnerable to sin. The stories in the Bible are not mere accounts of interesting and important historical events. They are dependable signage to help voyagers in every age navigate a dangerous path. Those who seek to discredit the Bible as a valid guide for life on Earth do so at their misguided peril.

15

Job's Affliction

Although the book of Job is positioned later in the Bible, the main character lived before the first accredited authors. Scholars propose that Job lived a few generations after Abraham. The content and structure of Job are unrivaled in ancient literature and attest to man's early intellectual prowess. They also hint at the foundational nature of man's spiritual orientation.

In early times historical accounts and genealogies were passed orally to succeeding generations. They were so widely known and commonly communicated that they were familiar to virtually everyone in a given community. Archeology has revealed that around 2000 BC the Babylonians and Sumerians recited poems called "A Man and His God", and "Praise to the God of Wisdom", that parallel Job. In comparison they read like comic books.

Because of a genealogical reference to Jobab in Genesis 36, some argue that Job may have been the second Edomite king, which would make him a great-great-grandson of Abraham and Sarah. Names mentioned in Genesis 36 appear in the book of Job. Job was probably a grandson of Esau and may have lived through the famine that overtook Israel and forced them into Egypt.

The land of Uz is thought to have been located between Egypt and Babylon along a caravan route near the Euphrates River. References to Job have been unearthed east of the Sea of Galilee. Once thickly populated as evidenced by the ruins of hundreds of ancient cities and villages, this region was known for the mineral rich soil in its fertile valleys.

Job, like Abraham and other Bible characters, is traditionally viewed from a materialistic perspective. Some analyze Job's mental, emotional and physical struggles, but Job is best studied for its straightforward religious and moral teaching. The aim of Job is not to provide geographical, scientific or historical information but to offer spiritual insight and guidance.

Job was a highly revered tribal chieftain of immense wealth and influence. He had seven sons and three daughters, and his possessions were such that he was called, "the greatest of all men of the east." That could also have been translated, "the most exemplary man among Semites." The Bible communicates that such a life of industry, honor, and personal integrity pleased God but begged the argument that a man's devotion to God could be based on his perceived blessings from God.

The book opens with a conversation between God and Satan, though neither God nor Satan is a physical being and they were not in a physical location. The point is well made that Job was a tremendously devout man who was critically concerned for his children's right standing before God. He prayed daily for each one individually and offered sacrifices in the event one of them might have sinned and dishonored God then neglected to personally repent.

When struck with the sudden loss of flocks and herds, personal property, health, and even his family, Job questioned God but remained faithful. Friends offered arguments people routinely use to explain suffering. They suggested God may have sent tragedy to punish Job for his secret sins or to discipline him. Job's aching nagging wife urged him to abandon the object of his admiration and worship that she argued let him down.

Job knew his heart, and questioned why a just and loving God would allow such distress to fall upon a righteous man. He pleaded for death, then for mercy, and then for understanding. Finally, he resolved to face his trials with courage to match his conviction and asked God to carry him through his many painful afflictions.

Job recognized and declared everyone's existence is a mystery beyond knowing and concluded that no matter what he was subjected to on Earth, his life was in the hands of God. When God finally revealed himself to Job, he did not offer a reason for suffering, but restored him many times over and blessed him for his faithfulness. Job's contentment in life did not depend on exterior circumstances, what he had or what he did, but upon his internal state of being. His relationship with God was appropriate and strong, so his ultimate security and peace were impenetrable.

Job addressed the age old question, "Why do the just have to suffer?" The obvious answer is we can't know. But the underlying answer from the opening chapters of Job coupled with the opening chapters of Genesis is that evil has infiltrated our existence and contends with God's perfect design. God is the source of life. Everything thrives in his presence. Apart from God, contamination leads to malady, brokenness, illness, or whatever you choose to call such a condition. Spiritual compromise, also properly referred to as sin, always ultimately leads to death.

Job was contaminated by the evil that existed in the world around him. He was inoculated when God mercifully injected himself into the situation to restore him. We are born into a world where the conduit that connects our physical beings to the source of life has been severed. When sin breaks the fragile cord that sustains us, we need a bridge. God must inject himself, and we must stop contending for control. Like a bone once broken, or a scar from a wound, the repair is stronger than the prior condition.

In Job we learn true wisdom does not come from intellectual understanding, but from acquiescing to God and the fullness of his completed plan. Anything we can dissect and analyze is but a small part of a much grander creation that we can never fully comprehend, and often discount in the name of man's inferior logic. Those who doubt the sovereignty of God have simply stopped looking beyond what they themselves can understand or master in order to accept. Pretending to be wise we make ourselves out to be fools. The wisdom of men will perish. God's blueprint overrides it and will ultimately prevail.

Part 3

Jewish Law Established

16

The Coming of Moses

Over the course of hundreds years of Egyptian captivity, Israel flourished even in bondage. Once independent aliens taking up temporary residence to survive a famine, they became slaves in a strange land in which they didn't belong. Their culture recognized and reinforced virtues of industry, integrity, ambition, and devotion to God and family above all. No matter where they found themselves, Israel prospered.

A Pharaoh of Egypt was providentially inspired to provide safe haven and nurturing for the developing nation in its infancy. Generations later, the Jews were caught off-guard when suddenly a different Pharaoh subjected them to slavery after they stayed and swelled to threaten his rule. Though Egypt came to enjoy and perhaps rely on slave labor, yet another Pharaoh sought to destroy this cohesive band of outsiders that continued to thrive against all efforts to break their solidarity when the threat grew to be disquieting. That Pharaoh ordered Egyptian midwives to kill every Jewish male at birth to thin their ranks.

One pious Hebrew mother had a son without employing midwives and secretly nursed him for three months. Fearing the child might be discovered and put to death, she placed him in a papyrus covered basket among the reeds along the Nile River. Pharaoh's daughter discovered the basket while bathing in the river and took pity on the young boy she assumed was orphaned. The princess's father agreed to let her raise him.

The princess saw a young Jewish girl nearby. Not knowing the girl was Moses' sister, Miriam, and that she had been watching after him, the princess asked if she knew of a Hebrew woman who could nurse him and help raise him. Of course the young girl recommended her mother, and the princess was none the wiser. The Bible says, "He became her son, and she called him Moses." Neither ancient Hebrew nor ancient Egyptian employed written vowels. In Egypt "msy" denoted a birth or adoption, and "ms" designated a boy. When Pharaoh Tutankhamun, colloquially referred to as King Tut, was a baby he would have been called Tut-mosée. Similarly, two consonants pronounced "mo-sheh" meant to extract or lure in Hebrew.

Moses grew up in the royal palace as a son of privilege. He was exposed to the best mentors and tutors. He learned to read and write. He mastered the military arts and learned how to govern. Egypt was already known for its great libraries and arenas. It was the cultural and economic hub of its time. Moses was quite educated and sophisticated, but he also knew and valued his Hebrew roots.

When he was forty years old, Moses encountered an Egyptian overseer beating a Hebrew slave. He intervened and ended up killing the overseer as the slave fled. Seeing no one around, Moses buried the body of his victim in a shallow grave and slipped away. When word reached the ears of Pharaoh he was furious and Moses ran away into the Sinai desert. He kept going until he reached Midea along the eastern shore of the Gulf of Aqaba. There, he met and married Zipporah, the daughter of Reuel, known as Jethro the high priest of Midea in his native tongue. Moses spent the next forty years learning to be a shepherd and supervise a nation of nomads.

Jethro was a descendant of Abraham by his second wife Keturah the Hamite, whom he married after Sarah died. The fact that Jethro was a priest and head cleric indicates that he remained faithful to the God of Abraham and could have helped Moses piece together his ancestry and better understand his cultural and religious heritage.

When Moses was eighty years old he encountered God in the form of a bush that seemed to burn but was not consumed by the fire. Moses heard a voice call out, "I have heard the cry of my people who are in Egypt." There God commissioned Moses to return to Egypt and bring Israel back to Canaan to fulfill his covenant with Abraham, Isaac, and Jacob. Unlike generations of Jews in Egypt, Moses likely traveled to Canaan with Jethro who would have gone there periodically to buy goods or meet with other dignitaries. Moses heard the stories of his homeland that were passed down to his mother as he grew up. He had probably seen the Promised Land and knew the route his father-in-law took through the Sinai Desert.

No longer confident, Moses protested that the task was too dangerous and that he had not spoken Hebrew or Egyptian for forty years. God assured Moses that he was able to provide for his safety and since he was self-conscious about his speech, his brother Aaron could assist and speak for him. When Moses still expressed reluctance, imploring, "Why would they listen to me?" God identified himself.

People had called God by various monikers based on how they experienced him. They called God El Shaddai which meant God is all powerful, Jehovah Rapha which meant source of healing, or Jehovah Jirah which meant source of provision. The Bible lists dozens of such names, all of which are simply translated "God" in our present Bible, but only once did God reveal who He really is. God instructed Moses to tell those he encountered that, "I am I am" sent him. Breaking down the structure of the phrase, variously translated "I am that I am", "I am who I am", "I am what I am", or "I am as I am", God didn't propose that he is sovereign because of what he has or what he does, but because of what He is. It's not a matter of position, possession, activity, or accomplishment. God is a state of being. And that state of being has jurisdiction over everything in the created order.

"Made in God's image" is not a matter of physical accomplishment or intellectual development. A man does not reflect God's likeness by what he acquires or achieves in his lifetime, but simply by coming to reflect God at the core of his being. Even a child can do that.

As Moses crossed the desert on his way back to Egypt, he encountered his brother, Aaron, who was simultaneously inspired to come in search of Moses. The improbable encounter in the middle of a barren wilderness reassured both of them. Moses shared his experience at the bush. Aaron explained the nudge in Goshen. Together they confidently returned to Egypt.

17

Plagues on Pharaoh's Gods

When Moses and Aaron returned to Egypt to demand that Pharaoh release the Hebrew slaves, they were not well received. The Israelites had seen that aggravating their elite rulers only led to harsher treatment. Abuse of conscripted slaves under Thothmes III, Ramses II, Amenhotep II, and Merneptah has been well documented. Israel arrived with 72 people. If the average couple had six children, given a lifespan of sixty, in 220 years they would have swelled to over 2 million among a native population estimated to have been seven million. Perhaps one fourth of the population of Egypt consisted of Jewish slave labor. The Jews posed a serious economic threat.

In the period from 1800 to 1400 BC Egypt grew to be a dominant empire. Upon Israel's departure Egypt declined and has remained a second tier world power. No record of Israel's exodus has been found, but there are no records of Egyptian defeats in the reigns of 21 kings during two dynasties that ruled from 1500 to 1200 BC. Perhaps an ancient account of one nation's triumphs and failings is more credible than another nation's controlled, and probably scrubbed, official historic record.

Moses and Aaron were sons of Amram the Levite priest. Moses was raised by a Queen of Egypt. As her firstborn son by adoption he was in line for a royal appointment. A rank of Prime Minister, like that of Joseph, would certainly have been in order. Scholars suggest that Moses was commander of the Army of the South when he fled to Midea at the age of forty.

Aaron, three years older than Moses, was a leader among his people. Upon their return, Aaron convinced the council of elders to support his brother's bid. Moses knew palace protocol and gained an audience with the new Pharaoh, who must have been keenly interested in seeing his long lost relative. At their first meeting Aaron asked Pharaoh to allow the people of Israel to go into the wilderness for a time of joint celebration and worship. Pharaoh refused and dismissed the notion that Moses and Aaron invoked the will of the true and living God, saying, "Who is your God that I should listen to him?"

To illustrate the power of God, Aaron threw down Moses' rod and it became a serpent. Pharaoh called on the priests of Nechebt, represented by a serpent. They threw their rods down too, but Aaron's serpent devoured them. When Aaron grabbed his serpent it became a rod again. Moses invoked a plague upon Egypt and God smote the Nile River, worshipped through Khnum and Hapi, guardian spirits of the Nile. It flowed like a stream of blood. People couldn't drink from it, bathe in it, or wash in it. Fish died and floated to its banks. Yet, Pharaoh would not relent. He attributed the miraculous event to a natural phenomenon and tried to rationalize it away, much as intelligent atheists do today.

Egyptian priests prayed to Heka for relief. Statues of Heka had the head of a frog. The next day frogs leapt from the Nile by the thousands. People couldn't walk on a crowded street or turn in their beds without landing on a frog. Pharaoh's priests appealed to the catlike goddess, Bast, only to be overrun with fleas, ticks, or lice in every house and public building. Pharaoh again stubbornly refused to let the Hebrews go and his priests turned to Apis, a god cast in the image of a bull. Flies swarmed so thick that people kept their mouths shut lest they swallow one. They then turned to Amon represented by a cow, and his wife, the goddess Mut, in the form of a vulture. Cattle throughout Egypt fell dead in the fields. Worldly Pharaoh again rationalized and called it a curious livestock epidemic.

The Egyptians turned to Seth, the earth god. Moses and Aaron countered their prayer and featherlike ashes from burn piles ascended to drift in the wind. People were beset with boils and skin sores wherever the ashes landed. With each plague Pharaoh begged Moses to ask God to remove the curse and vowed to let the Jews go. Each time a curse was lifted Pharaoh found a rational explanation and retracted his promise, as secular leaders still do.

Moses warned Pharaoh that hail would destroy the crops of Egypt and kill any creature that didn't have ample cover. Nut, the sky goddess, and Serapis, the god of fire, water, and rain, proved impotent to stop it. The land was stripped of crops and vegetation. The entire season was lost. When locusts swarmed to consume the diminished harvest of wheat and rye, Isis, the goddess of life, was of no consequence.

Because Pharaoh refused to see what should have been obvious, Moses declared that God would blanket the land in darkness. The priests called upon their powerful sun god, Ra, to no avail. Egyptians were held captive in their houses while visibility was impaired for three days and nights. The Bible says God hardened Pharaoh's heart. But God did not decide for Pharaoh, nor impose his will. Rather, each time Pharaoh antagonized God his heart grew more calloused and less receptive. God merely allowed the design of the nature he created to run its course. Deaf to God, Pharaoh was afforded one last opportunity to listen to someone who communicated with God and could ascertain his will.

Life stems from God who created it, and death ensues where God cannot freely flow. That is the clear premise of the Bible from the onset. Pharaoh would either repent to recalibrate and align himself with the God of creation, or face the natural consequence of his rebellion. Moses proclaimed the angel of death would visit every household in the land and confiscate every firstborn among humans and domesticated animals as recompense for sinful defiance.

God gave life and made men stewards over his creation. God admonished men to procreate and execute his will on Earth. God adequately demonstrated that He alone reigns supreme. Depending on any other god, even a material resource, was shown to be pure folly. Those who refuse to acknowledge God today share Pharaoh's disposition, and thus his fate. Their hearts grow more calloused through the trials they don't allow to awaken them, and they put at risk what they should value most; life itself.

Pharaoh thought himself a god. He believed that by his own creative logic he sustained his life and commanded his resources. Every man has the same tendency. Now, the true and living God would make a statement to resound throughout the ages. Pharaoh mocked, "Who is your God that I should listen to him?" Paradoxically, Pharaoh himself would soon show the rest of us why we should listen and conform. God is dependably patient, but He cannot be mocked.

18

Passover and Exodus

A year passed since Moses' return to Egypt. Plagues occasioned by Pharaoh's willful defiance had taken a toll and made an impression. Moses now stood out prominently among anxious Egyptian citizens and cowering Hebrew slaves alike. Those who once doubted, at last took reverent notice of the God of Israel. The nation of promise who strayed and became slaves, indifferent to their religion, were hopeful again.

The people of God were being called home, but an obstinate ruler of an oppressive nation refused to comply. The first plagues were universal. Later plagues were more severe, but had no impact in the land of Goshen where the Israelites settled and continued to prosper. The message could not have been clearer. Pharaoh subjected those under his charge to great hardship, and even loss of life. But as heads of their households, the men of Egypt were guilty too, for not rising up to demand prudence from their leaders, much less justice for the godly people in their midst. This set the stage for a confrontation that would command everyone's attention and finally break those who continued to shun God.

Moses approached Pharaoh to demand that every Hebrew be released from his bondage. Pharaoh dismissed him. But before leaving, Moses announced that as defiant men renounce the God of their creation and retract their sacred promises, so the God of life would reciprocate and renounce those He created by retracting his most sacred gift to them. The angel of death would pass through the land to reclaim the lives of firstborn sons of every household that did not bow to God and repent.

Moses advised God honoring people in Goshen and throughout Egypt that before the sun set on the fourteenth day after the new moon of the first month of the new year they were to kill and roast a lamb and paint the lintel and door posts of their houses with its blood to signify their allegiance to God. Households throughout Israel complied. This would be every Jew's last supper in the land of their hardship and bondage. They worked diligently and solemnly commemorated their imminent freedom. Across Egypt, those in homes where the blood was not prominently displayed paid an eternal price.

Pharaoh woke to learn that his firstborn son, the heir to his earthly kingdom, died in the night. Pharaoh wailed and lamented, but there was nothing he could do. Likewise, screams of anguish rang out across the land. Every Egyptian family that turned a deaf ear to God's prophet suffered the same fate. The battered citizens at last rose up, and Pharaoh was compelled to let God's people go.

The Hebrews collected gold, jewelry, and livestock from Egyptian natives upon their departure. There was no just recompense, but those who suppressed them and grew comfortable at the slaves' expense were genuinely contrite. Pharaoh, at last, was broken. The people of God who had been preparing for a full year were ready. They left the only home they had known that very day.

Six hundred thousand men above the age of twenty, along with their women, children, and all of their meager belongings formed a human caravan several miles long and walked out of bondage into a world that was totally unknown and unfamiliar to them. There were Egyptians among them who saw the hand of God and longed to join the Hebrews and convert to their ways.

Days passed and strong-willed Pharaoh changed his mind yet again. He gathered his army and gave chase by chariot. By now the Israelites had made it to the Sea of Reeds along the trade route on the way to Sinai. Moses raised his arms to hoist his staff and the people he led marched across the wide swampy riverbed that once connected the Bitter Lakes to the Gulf of Suez that opens into the Red Sea and flows into the Indian Ocean.

They crossed on dry ground while a wall of fire and smoke miraculously rolled in to impede the advancing enemy troops and obscure their view. When the cloud lifted, Pharaoh ordered his soldiers to massacre the entire lot of vulnerable defenseless Jews, but as they crossed in chase the wheels of their chariots got tangled in the reeds. They were stalled as the tide swept back in to engulf and drown those who were in pursuit. Frustrated, humiliated and defeated, Pharaoh conceded and finally withdrew.

Instead of leading the people directly into the promised land by way of the coastal route known as the Way of the Philistines or using the inland merchant route called the Way of Shur, Moses led his people south into Sinai, back to the mountain where he had encountered the burning bush that set him to his divine task. At Mount Sinai, seven weeks into their journey, God gave Moses ten critical commands written on tablets of stone. Those laws comprised the timeless foundation for governing men's conduct on Earth. Jews still celebrate the holiday of Shavuot that we know as Pentecost fifty days after the Passover feast to commemorate the reading of the Law as it was first delivered at Mount Sinai.

The family of Israel became an independent nation of tribal clans, but the nation was neither devoted to, nor disciplined toward God. Rather, they were as willful and self-centered as every generation that preceded or followed them. They were not able to maintain an orientation beyond their human circumstances and natural surroundings. Even while Moses received the Law in close communion with God on the mountain, the masses below slipped back into debauchery and idol worship.

When Moses observed their folly upon his descent, he vented his frustration by hurling, and in-so-doing destroying, the initial tablets of the law. Yet, he graciously interceded on the people's behalf when God proposed to eradicate the entire population and rebuild a favored nation through Moses alone, as he had done with Noah and Abraham. The Bible illustrates, and Moses understood, that people who have lived in broken fellowship, apart from the God of their creation, do not readily bend their will and are not easily recalibrated and restored.

Thousands who defied God and rebuffed his servant, Moses, died on that day. Those who were saved and experienced God as their sole provider, protector, prosecutor and sovereign Lord aligned behind Moses to follow the mysterious cloud which took the form of a pillar of smoke by day, and a glowing column of fire by night. Together they marched to their ancestral promised land.

19

Laws to Live By

Upon their arrival in Egypt in the mid-nineteenth century BC, Israel was a close knit family of seventy-two people. They kept to themselves in a region called Goshen a few miles north of the city of Heliopolis in the district of On, where Jacob's son Joseph lived. A little south along the Nile River laid Giza, home to pyramids and tombs of pharaohs. A few miles further stood the once capitol city of Noph, more widely known as Memphis. On the northern border of Goshen, Jewish slaves would build the great city of Rameses.

Upon their arrival, Jacob and his family were welcomed as honored guests. They were granted access to some of the best grazing land in Egypt, and afforded the freedom to live and worship however they chose. They abided by the laws of Egypt that Mizraim the Hamite established and pharaohs subsequently codified over the nation's long history, dating back to a few decades after the great flood of Noah's time.

Jacob brought his family to Egypt three years into a severe seven year famine. Jacob's sons vowed to return to their homeland of Canaan immediately after the famine and promised to bury their father beside his father, Isaac, and grandfather, Abraham. As it turned out, Jacob died in Egypt and his sons carried him to Canaan as promised. But they returned to Egypt and put down roots that would be their undoing over the next couple of centuries.

No one can say what would have become of the children of Israel had they simply kept their word and followed the will of their father who made a pact with God. Had they proliferated in Canaan they would have, in all likelihood, still kept to themselves and devoted themselves to living in accordance with divine guidance. They may have established an exemplary godly nation in the midst of hostile neighbors who might have come to see how they were blessed for adhering to God's sovereignty. That was, after all, God's original call upon Abram. By pursuing what seemed logical and expedient to them instead of honoring the old covenant God made with their forefathers, they failed their patriarchs and enslaved future generations. Human failures are often the substance of divine lessons.

God gave Abraham a simple charge, "Submit to my will and I will bless you." The more thorough the submission, the greater the blessing would be. God imparted the same charge to Isaac, and then to Jacob. It's the charge He gave Adam and Noah, and it is the opportunity He affords to each person who opens his heart to God today.

Upon their departure from Egypt, Moses shared that charge with a nation of two and a half million people who endured years of bondage because their ancestors veered from the will of God. Now, by their own humble submission, they experienced miraculous salvation when the angel of death passed over their homes. This generation was finally enlightened. Yet, they too were blinded by a truth they could not, or would not, accept. They closed their eyes and insisted on having their own way. Willfulness, discontent, and rebellion persisted in their ranks while they lived under, and depended on, the clear and present cloud of God's blessing.

Dare we point a finger? Given freedom, men naturally seek independence. Given guidance, men naturally seek rules; from which they then seek exceptions. The only law men really need to know is, "Submit to God and He will bless you." But even knowing that, we drift; employing our own logic to establish our own will in our own strength on a short-sighted personal quest for pleasure, possessions, or prominence.

In the Garden of Eden God gave man both guidance and freedom. He divulged his will without imposing it. We are stewards in God's physical universe. To please God, love God. To love God, be a good steward. To be a good steward, do God's bidding. To do God's bidding, make His garden a better place. To make His garden a better place, simply enhance what is growing properly and cut what needs to be pruned.

In order to facilitate ethical living and moral relationships God provided his people with Ten Commandments. The famous commandments are listed in Exodus and Deuteronomy with slight variations. They are the underpinning for 613 very specific regulations established by early legalistic Jews.

The first four commandments govern every man's union with God. First, we must acknowledge that the God of creation is our ultimate source and the only true and living God. Second, we are to refrain from worshipping anything we have the capacity to construct, mold, or manipulate. Distraction from our true God is the essence of sin. Third, we must never discount the reality, relevance, or authority of God. God cannot be mocked! And fourth, we are to set aside a time of quiet reflection, refreshment, and restoration. We need regular routine recalibration to our source, lest we stray.

The last six commandments direct human activity in the material world. Respect and honor the traditions and ways of your ancestors in order to extend civil society. Value and preserve human life. Be faithful to your vows and hold your family bond sacred. Don't take or use what doesn't belong to you without the owner's permission. Don't speak of someone to his detriment without necessity or legal cause. Don't covet what someone else has, or wish you could trade places, but deal with the present reality God has assigned you for his purpose and your own good.

Jesus Christ taught the Torah as expressed in Deuteronomy, "The greatest commandment is to love the Lord your God with every thought, feeling, and effort. Then to back that up with substance, go about making life better for other people." The simple straightforward benchmark question becomes: How much do you love God as demonstrated in the lives of the people you have an opportunity to affect?

20

Generational Detour

More than a year lapsed from the time Moses left Mount Sinai after his exposure to a bush that burned but wasn't consumed. God used Moses to usher Israel out of Egypt like an unruly flock of sheep. The shepherd had his hands full. This is probably as good a picture as we have of our own behavior before an all-seeing God whose care for us is hampered by our own lack of divine insight and responsiveness.

In Egypt God looked on millions of people who must have sensed they were caught up in something they weren't designed for in a place they didn't belong. However, the people of God grew accustomed to their alien surroundings and complacent with their lot. They called Egypt home, tended to demands of daily life, and acquiesced to their destiny. Like us, they couldn't see beyond life as they experienced it in a world as they understood it. And like them, we blindly wonder why we're confined and oppressed if there really is a God who loves us. We give passing misdirected thought to what lies beyond in a realm we were formed in and made for, but have become contentedly detached from.

God cannot cohabit with sin because sin, by definition, entails separation from God. Men live on Earth comfortably, but no one could approach the Sun without being consumed. For us to think we can live a carnal life and cuddle up to deity is ludicrous. We don't come to God on our terms, and God does not approach us without burning up what doesn't belong in his presence. The refining fire confined to the bush at Sinai was at work in the hearts of Israel.

When Moses scaled Mount Sinai a second time, it appeared to those looking on from below that the entire summit was ablaze. It's hard to believe that anyone who personally observed the plagues in Egypt, experienced deliverance from a life of bondage, escaped annihilation at the hand of a formidable army, and viewed the spectacle of a burning mountain could question God, grumble, and defiantly seek to gratify his lusts. But, that is the essence of man depicted in the Bible and in the annals of history. In honesty, it's your story and mine.

Plants with shallow roots wither quickly. People with shallow spiritual roots easily resort to physical means. The Jews quickly and easily reverted to their old ways. Like orphaned children with wayward tendencies, they needed both encouragement and discipline. Uprooting and replanting an unhealthy damaged plant takes effort and patience. A lot of limbs needed to be discarded to save the plant and make it flower again.

The one God planted in paradise and called Adam, the Hebrew word for mankind, proved unworthy of His garden. Shoots from Adam spread out to dominate, but strangled what they were designed to accent and support. Through droughts and floods; left unattended or oppressed; inbred or exposed to hybrids; securely potted or allowed to blossom in foreign fields; God monitored His creation to ensure the progress of the design He engineered from the beginning.

Upon laying down the law in stone, so to speak, a revolt erupted. In Moses short absence, willful people ate, did, and even worshipped what they were expressly instructed to avoid. Discipline ensued and punitive action restored order and respect. A nation of rebellious children learned to live according to healthy structure and immutable rules. The Jews at last set out from Sinai for the Promised Land, marching in organized ranks by families within clans within tribes. Jacob's descendants were going home after a four hundred year diversion wherein they swelled from 72 people to over two million. They had left a family farm, now they needed a much larger estate. Home had a bigger meaning.

Upon reaching the border of the territory they claimed by eternal edict from the very God who fashioned it and bequeathed it to their forefathers, Moses sent tribal leaders to scout the land. Annual festivities of Baal worship drew foreigners from all quarters. Itinerant Jewish spies could have mingled in major cities throughout Canaan undetected. Representatives from ten of the twelve tribes brought back dismal reports. "They're huge," one conveyed. "We're like grasshoppers next to them," Another shared. "There's no way we can penetrate their fortified walled cities. They're seasoned warriors. They have iron chariots. They're too sophisticated for us to contend with." On and on, they groaned. In short, they weren't willing to proceed, though God had assured them of ultimate victory.

Caleb from the tribe of Ephraim proposed, "God brought us here and He has declared what we must do. That's enough for me. Now let's advance and watch God work on our behalf." Joshua from the tribe of Judah stood alone with Caleb. When the common people rallied behind the pessimists, God determined they were not worthy to claim the inheritance set aside for them. Instead, the Jews were compelled to wander aimlessly for forty years until those above the age of twenty died in the wilderness they seemed to prefer. Among their peers, only Caleb and Joshua ultimately lived to claim their inheritance in the Promised Land.

God miraculously provided adequate food and water for their daily consumption. They camped around a mysterious cloud of smoke each day that turned into a pillar of fire at night. Where the pillar moved, the camp followed because God demanded to remain at the core of Israel. God gave Moses the design for a worship tent that was always erected under the pillar in the middle of the camp. Throughout their sojourn, God dictated laws and edicts that Moses scribed and presented to the people.

On the eve of crossing the Jordan River into Canaan, Moses scaled Mount Nebo to behold the fertile valley with flowing rivers and rolling hills. He beheld the Promised Land, but would never enter. Instead, God granted him an immortal ending.

Moshe's name, meaning drawn out, was fortuitous in regard to being extracted from the Nile when he was an infant, and drawing water from the well at Midea when he was welcomed into Jethro's family at forty. Forty years later he drove the slaves out of Egypt and crossed the Sea of Reeds. Then, after forty more years, God drew him up into Mount Nebo, never to return. His life spanned 120 years; twelve decades in different capacities in three distinct phases of forty years apiece.

21

Joshua and the Judges

When Israel crossed into Canaan they lacked the modern weapons developed during the Iron Age; the bow, battering ram, and war chariot to name a few. Leaders inside the walled city of Jericho must have worried, and chuckled, when over a million people surrounded them and started marching and singing hymns. For six days Israelites paraded behind their priests, blowing horns at the city. On the seventh day, the walls collapsed.

British archeologists uncovered six foot thick wall blocks at Jericho in the 1950s. Much of the wall was dated from more than six thousand years ago and consisted of nothing more than packed mud; hardly more than a cosmetic deterrent. Jericho was well suited to shepherds, but better farmland lay to the north. Israel occupied Jericho and confidently set out to conquer the fertile hill country to the north.

In Israel's long absence, Canaan was variously occupied by Hittites, Hivites, Ammonites, Jebusites, Philistines, Moabites, Edomites, Perrizites, Girgashites, and a host of tribes descended from Ishmael, Esau, and Lot, as well as other clans of Hamites who settled there. War-lords regularly ascended and were conquered and territories changed hands routinely.

In excavations at Gezer, archeologists found the stratum of 1500 BC that immediately preceded Israel's occupation. They uncovered ruins of a temple that had been used for worshipping Baal and Ashtoreth and found remains of infants who had been sacrificed. Another abomination concerned the practice of killing a child to bury his corpse in a wall or floor of a new residence to bring good fortune to the rest of the family. In villages across the region findings confirmed these and other hideous practices. There was, and there remains, a stunted view of human life among many in the region.

Statuary of explicit poses and exaggerated organs depict rampant sexual indulgence associated with idol worship of the period. These discoveries help civilized people better understand why the God of the Bible commanded the armies of Joshua to conquer the land, kill its inhabitants, and destroy their shrines and cities. Such perversion and brutality bring to mind God's intervention in Noah's time, and at Sodom and Gomorrah. Such a perspective could guide men well in the present age.

God calls men to innocence, but not naivety. Naïve people yearn for redemption and restoration without discerning others' willful destructive intent. Those who are wise understand that innocence must be preserved by the expulsion of evil and avoidance of corruption. The crux of the Bible's message is that righteousness, defined as right standing with God, leads to life, and sin, defined as separation from God, leads to death. Those who defy God invite calamity. Those in their midst who turn a blind eye share their fate. God is not so cruel He would destroy the compliant, but is so just He allows all men to choose their own fate. Adam and Eve, like you and me, were seduced by evil in their midst. Wisdom beckons us to honor God and purge the space we occupy.

After most rival kingdoms were uprooted, Joshua, to whom Moses passed his scepter, oversaw the distribution of land to the twelve tribes that constituted the nation of Israel. Joshua's great failing was that he didn't completely destroy the perverse tribes he conquered as God instructed. Though Israel vowed to honor God and follow his laws and statutes, a remnant of native Canaanites survived to reinstate their deities and resume their repugnant practices.

For a time Israel lived at peace among her Canaanite neighbors. By design, Israel had no strong central government. Twelve independent tribes worshipped a common God, promoting individual liberty and personal accountability. Occasionally, strife broke out and military strategists referred to as Judges rose to squelch insurgences. Othniel of the tribe of Judah fought off the Mesopotamians. Ehud of Benjamin contended with the Moabites, Ammonites, and Amalekites. Shamgar fought the Philistines.

Deborah of Ephraim, the first and only woman Judge, organized a coalition of tribes to take control of the prized Jezreel Valley. She sent her military commander, Barak, to face Sisera and his 900 iron chariots at the base of Mount Tabor. The Israelites were greatly disadvantaged, but when Sisera gave the order to attack, a sudden downpour bogged the Canaanite chariots in mud and Israeli foot soldiers made short work of their adversary.

Gideon from the tribe of Manasseh took the reins from Deborah and staved off the Mideanites and the Amalekites. Moses once lived among the Mideanites who descended from Abraham and Keturah, the dark skinned Hamite princess that Abraham married after Sarah died. Moses married a daughter of Jethro the priest of Midea. But over time the Mideanites fully integrated into the culture of idol worship that pervaded the Arabian Peninsula. When massive armies invaded, the Israelites hid their grain and lived in mountain caves.

Gideon summoned the Israelites to face the Arabians at the base of Mount Moreh. As his prospective army of 3,000 assembled at the stream that flowed from the mountain, he watched each soldier get a drink. Spry young men comfortably bent down to lap up all they wanted. But stiff and sore from their journey, elderly warriors knelt on one knee, cupped a hand, and brought water to their lips. God led Gideon to call up 300 older warriors who were still devout and motivated to die for their sacred values and send the rest home so all would know that if they won the battle it was by the hand of God. Their miraculous victory was so extensive the enemy retreated, never to return.

Joshua's son, Abimelech, a half-breed, was a corrupt inept city-king who lasted only a few years. He was followed by Tola of Issachar, and Jair of Manasseh. They judged at a time of relative peace. Jephtah from Manasseh stood against the Amalekites and the Philistines, as did Ibzin of Judah, Elon of Zebulun, and Abdon of Ephraim.

We tend to think of judges as people who preside over courts and adjudicate laws. The term in Hebrew depicts an avenger. Enterprises and institutions; be they social, legal, military, or religious; are viable and helpful. But the Bible suggests that God creates each person with an eternal soul that is independently capable of relating to his creator.

God periodically inspires and raises up people in our midst to contend for righteousness, govern righteously, or restore righteous order. We benefit from a righteous leader's devotion and efforts, but each of us is accountable to God for purging ourselves. God calls you and me to contend with evil in our midst, govern ourselves honorably, and restore sacred order. God calls all of us to purity. He supernaturally inspires and empowers some of us to purify.

22

Samson and Delilah

Though a few others arose, Samson from the tribe of Dan was the last major Judge in Israel. When lands were parceled to the twelve tribes of Israel after they crossed the Jordan River, the clan of Dan was assigned the fertile coastal plain occupied by the Philistines. Theirs was arguably one of the most enviable inheritances. But they never purged the land, so they never acquired the blessing.

Over ensuing decades Dan produced great warriors and even effective judges. They won great battles, but they were tentative and compromised, so in the end they lost the war, and hence their posterity. Though victory was assured by God and pronounced by prophets, the people of Dan lacked faith. Ultimately, they were displaced from their territory and forced to settle outside the northern border of what originally constituted the "land of promise" their brothers occupied. Their history is our admonition.

Christians who scoff at the radical ideology of ISIL, the Islamic State in the Levant, need to consider their premise and reevaluate. Though we differ with their theology and their means, we must concede to their objective and devotion. They know that allowing infidels among them will ultimately lead to compromise and break their caliphate. Their leaders taunt us saying they are more dedicated to die for Allah than we are to live for Christ.

Though they occupied the lands, no tribe of Israel thoroughly purged their territory of wicked influences that later brought them down. Instead, they acquiesced. In the name of compassion they allowed those who were young, innocent, or disadvantaged to live among them. For the sake of political correctness, they allowed people of differing opinions and backgrounds to practice their alien ways. They grew comfortable with or overlooked issues and behaviors that were clearly counter to their values and culture. Over time, adversaries in their midst grew stronger and bolder.

Before they were expelled, Dan was subjugated to the very people they should have dominated. Their charge was not simply to take up residence in the land, but to eradicate evil influences. Because they chose to allow Philistines to coexist alongside them, they were eventually overcome by the forces they were to have eliminated. Their soft-hearted, well-intentioned rationalization brought on their own oppression. God is ever-willing to intervene on our behalf, but then as now, He is reluctant to impose himself against our will.

Samson's elderly parents were among the devout minority. They consecrated their son to God when he was born and Samson lived under a Nazarite vow all his life. Under the vow he was obliged to abstain from eating grapes or drinking wine. He was to avoid contact with dead animals. And he could not cut his hair. But children cannot be bound by a parent's vow, and Samson did not adopt his parents' intimate faith in God. The boy who was dedicated to avenge God's people was not devoted to God.

The Bible portrays a young man with superhuman physical strength who lacked moral discipline. He grew up a spoiled bully who ate and drank and touched and took what he wanted. He spent a lot of his time in vineyards and reveling at parties. He killed predatory beasts and antagonistic men that crossed his path. No one could stop him. Samson was purported to have killed an attacking mountain lion with his bare hands and was credited with killing thousands of enemy soldiers in hand to hand combat, many with the jawbone of an ass he picked up when he dropped his sword.

He had an explosive temper and a weakness for beautiful women. One such woman was named Delilah, a Philistine. Though he ate grapes and drank wine, and even handled dead beasts and dead men, he never cut his hair. It was the only element of his vow to God that he had not violated.

When he revealed his secret to Delilah she sold the information to soldiers who were then able to cut his hair to sap his dignity and his strength. They subdued him as he slept, bound him, gouged his eyes out with a hot iron, and forced him to work as a pack animal.

They put him on display at a ceremony honoring their god, Dagon. A great crowd clamored to see mighty Samson chained between the two main pillars of their great temple. Philistine tribal leaders and dignitaries were present. The first and only prayer attributed to Samson came at the end of his life. Physically blind, his spiritual eyes at last were open. Samson prayed that God would grant him one last opportunity to serve his nation and his sovereign Lord. In the most colossal of his mighty endeavors, when he pulled the pillars of the great temple from their bases the roof came down and the walls collapsed, killing mighty Samson and virtually everyone inside.

Samson did not become weak because he lost his hair. His strength was never in his hair. Samson doomed himself when he forsook his vow and the supernatural power of God's Holy Spirit abandoned him. Do not disregard or take for granted the last strand of righteousness that keeps you tethered to God.

Two phrases resurface in the Bible each time a Judge passed on. The Bible discloses that the people reverted to their old ways and, "did that which was evil in the sight of the Lord." And at that time, "Everyone did that which seemed right in his own eyes." Now as then people rationalize and presume, and the Lord cannot be happy with what he observes.

Like Samson, people who have been blessed and should be consecrated to God exert their own will in their own strength in pursuit of their own agendas for their own gratification and enrichment. Like Samson, we see the world from a material perspective. God forbid we should be judged, oppressed, and humiliated before we open our spiritual eyes and do what God designed us for. You are here to do God's bidding. He has appointed your time and place and circumstance. Open your eyes and your ears to His Spirit.

23

The Story of Ruth

When yet another extended drought bore down on Israel, Elimelech, a Jew from Bethlehem, ran out of food and funds and was compelled to sell his land. Destitute and humiliated, he took his wife and two sons to Moab, east of the Dead Sea. Descended from Lot, Moabites were distant cousins to the Jews. They worshipped Chemosh and were among those whose rituals included infant sacrifice.

Elimelech died in Moab and his sons married local girls who converted to Judaism. When both men died a few years later, Elimelech's widow decided to go back home. Her doting daughters-in-law escorted her out of Moab, but Naomi pressed them to return home to their mothers and resume their Moabite ways. She had nothing to offer and knew they would fare better in their native culture.

Oprah agreed and reintegrated back into Moabite society. But Ruth insisted on going to Israel with the mother-in-law she had come to love and felt obligated to care for as long as she lived. "Don't ask me to leave you," she said, "Where you go, I will go. And I will reside with you wherever you dwell. Your people will be my people, and your God will be my God. I will die where you take me, and be buried alongside you." And she swore an oath before the Lord.

Realizing Ruth could not be persuaded otherwise, the pair set out for Bethlehem and arrived at the onset of the barley harvest. Her family and friends welcomed Naomi back home and warmly accepted her loyal daughter-in-law from Moab, who was clearly now a committed Jewess.

In need of food, Ruth eagerly volunteered to glean whatever was left after reapers harvested a field. It so happened the field she chose belonged to Boaz, a wealthy nephew of Elimelech. Boaz was a descendant of Rahab, the storied Canaanite who helped Joshua's army invade and conquer Jericho. She repented and converted to Judaism and was legendary for helping the Jews reestablish themselves in their promised land. Boaz was highly regarded in the land of Judah.

Boaz spotted Ruth and inquired about her. He learned that she married into his family in Moab and now cared for his first cousin's widow with whom she returned to Judah. He thanked Ruth for her devotion to Naomi and expressed his admiration for all that he heard about her. "Don't go to another field," he admonished. "Stay here and glean with my servants. I'll make sure you have plenty of food. And I've told my men not to bother you. You'll be safe and have ample to eat here."

When Ruth asked Boaz why he extended such kindness to an alien, he answered, "May the Lord reward you for what you have done in sacrificing for another. God will provide for you in this land you have entered into under his care and trust." She thanked him graciously, and he invited her to dine with his servants.

When Naomi learned what happened she informed Ruth that Boaz was a close kinsman. He was rewarding her in honor of relatives, living and dead. The providential hand of God led them to the most trustworthy and dependable source of provision they could have sought.

Naomi advised Ruth to do whatever Boaz suggested, and stay close to his other maidens. She said, "Trust me. I know our customs and culture. Boaz will winnow barley on his threshing floor tonight. Wash yourself, dress up, and put on perfume. Don't draw his attention, but inconspicuously observe where he lays down after he eats and drinks. Take his sandals off while he sleeps and lay at his feet. When he wakes he'll tell you what to do."

Boaz woke up in the night and was startled to discover Ruth at his feet. Her gesture put her at his disposal. Removing someone's sandals was reserved for slave servants and the closest of kin. Ruth was making herself available to Boaz. Instead of taking advantage of Ruth, Boaz lauded her innocent virtue and proposed to pursue the role of kinsman redeemer. When the head of a household died, a near kinsman could step into his role as father or husband, pay off debts, and adopt the family in the name of the deceased.

Boaz consulted the elders of the village and confronted the only other relative who might step in for Elimelech's family. Once there were no objecting contenders and he was assured there were no entanglements, Boaz bought back Elimelech's property and married Ruth in place of Elimelech's son Mahlon who was the last to die and could have inherited Elimelech's property rights. Boaz and Ruth bore a son to inherit the field in the name of Elimelech's lineage, and they called him Obed. Naomi was privileged to help raise him as his grandmother.

So Abraham had Isaac. Isaac had Jacob. Jacob had Judah. Judah had Pharez. Pharez had Hezron. Hezron had Ram. Ram had Amminadab. Amminadab had Nashon. Nashon had Salmon. Salmon had Boaz. Boaz had Obed. Obed would father Jesse. And Jesse would give rise to King David.

Archeologists have found a one room structure under the Church of the Nativity in Bethlehem that is said to have been the traditional home ceded to Boaz's son Obed, who gave it to his son Jesse, whose son David was probably born there. Ultimately, Jesus Christ was born in a borrowed space a short distance from that very place. Boaz's field from which Ruth gleaned and young David shepherded is adjacent to the traditional field where angels announced Jesus' birth to shepherds 1100 years later.

Part 4

Kings and Kingdoms

24

Israel's First King

For hundreds of years rag-tag militias of Hebrew volunteers defended themselves against neighboring warlord kings and their invading armies. Israel yearned for one among them to step up, take charge, unite them, and lead them into conquests. They longed to elevate their national stature. Lacking a strong leader they followed the natural course of people born with free will in a material world. The Bible says, "Every man did what was right in his own eyes."

Occasionally, prophets rose up to proclaim what God revealed to them through study and prayer, but a prophet's role was communicating God's wisdom and instruction, not executing it. Each person was accountable for his response when confronted with the sacred truth God funneled through His prophets who, by the way, weren't given any latitude. If what a Jewish prophet said proved to be untrue or something he predicted didn't happen, he was dishonored and stoned to death.

Samuel was the last official Judge of Israel. He was also revered by the masses as a prophet. The citizens of Israel beseeched Samuel to step aside and give them a king. They wanted a worldly king, like other nations, not a spiritual guide. Samuel advised them that allowing themselves to be ruled by anyone but God was a bad idea. He warned that a king would conscript their sons as soldiers and their daughters as servants. Kings ultimately impose taxes and confiscate the best lands for their own use. Nevertheless, a new generation lost sight of their ancestors' gradual decline into bondage. They sought security and comfort, and fell prey to the ploy of the devil to accommodate their own desire above God's design.

Samuel was providentially led to the tribe of Benjamin where he found Saul, the son of Kish, the chieftain of Gibeah. Saul was a proven warrior in his early thirties. He was unusually tall, handsome and intelligent. Normal Hebrews stood to the height of his shoulders. By shallow cultural standards of appearance, then as now, Saul looked to be a clear choice. Samuel reluctantly anointed him as the king apparent.

Soon afterward, the tribe of Manasseh fell under siege of the Amorites at Jabesh-Gilead. When the villagers sought terms of surrender, powerful King Nahash promised to spare their lives but said he would pluck out every man's right eye to disgrace Israel and brand the clan of Manasseh as his property. The elders of the tribe asked for time to consider and sent out an urgent plea. Saul heard their plea and mobilized a small army that rushed from the region of Benjamin to ambush the Amorites at neighboring Manasseh the following night. Saul's band routed the Amorites and ran them out of the country. Saul became an instant military hero. The people saw God's hand at work in him. Samuel, still dubious, officially crowned Saul and the people rejoiced.

Over the next two years Saul built an army of several thousand men and determined to eject the Philistines from the borders of Israel. He attacked a garrison at Geba a few miles north of his capital at Gibeah. Stationing two thousand trained soldiers to cut off troops that might come to their aid, Saul sent his son Jonathan to sack Geba with a thousand more. They wiped out the Philistine village.

The Philistines united to counter-attack at Michmash near Saul's capital, where ten thousand horsemen, chariots, and foot soldiers converged and Saul's army scattered. Saul was left with six hundred fighting men. Unknown to his father, Jonathan and his armor bearer sneaked up on a Philistine camp and ambushed them, killing them all. The Israelites rallied and chased thousands of Philistines that panicked and tried to flee. Their victory staved off the Philistines and emboldened the army of Israel.

Under Saul the Israelites chased the Amorites, Zobahites, and Arameans across their borders to the north. They ran the Ammonites across the Jordan valley to the east and pushed the Amalekites into the southern desert. But Samuel resented the peoples' demand for a human king, and he never warmed to Saul. He was dependably critical and condescending toward Israel's first earthly king. When Samuel was a week late arriving for a battle, Saul's soldiers threatened mutiny or desertion. Saul took it upon himself to make the customary priestly offering before venturing into war. Samuel never forgave that transgression. Despite his many efforts and successes, Saul never gained Samuel's respect or approval.

When the neighboring Amalekites flaunted their idolatry and uninhibited perversion, God inspired Samuel to instruct the army of Israel to tear down the strongholds of the wicked, demolish their shrines, and kill their inhabitants. Samuel told Saul the people of God were to purge the land God bequeathed to them of every vile influence that might tempt or divert them. But Saul spared the Amalekite king and looted his gold, silver, jewels and other valuables. Saul confiscated the best livestock for breeding, meals, and "sacred offerings".

Saul ignored Samuel's edict and pursued what he thought made more sense. In doing what he determined to be acceptable according to his human perspective, Saul inadvertently preserved the moral compromise that would come to destroy the nation he was entrusted to establish. True moral leadership advances God's will. Leaders who impose their own willful logic apart from seeking God's intent for their nation or group allow evil to infiltrate their ranks. Samuel angrily announced that another king would replace Saul.

Despite the paranoia and erratic behavior Saul exhibited through the rest of his reign, he proved to be an effective leader who established a strong military and governing foundation that allowed Israel to thrive for centuries. Like many modern politicians, Saul was a grand worldly statesman who lacked a strong spiritual foundation.

Despite the fact he was a devout man and a religious giant, Samuel was a person like the rest of us. He was given to emotional fits, his sons were lost to corruption, and he was jealous of another surpassing him. Every man, regardless of his station in life, has to suppress his natural thoughts and emotions to serve the will of God. The Bible illustrates that when judging another we should consider their carnal inclination and concede that everyone has potential weaknesses.

25

David and Goliath

Samuel was a popular prophet who viewed himself a benevolent priest and judge akin to ancient Melchizedek. He took it upon himself to establish his sons in the priesthood and granted them special privileges they routinely took advantage of for personal gain. Samuel's children did not inherit their father's devotion to God, and a life of ease and privilege proved to be their downfall. A man can influence his offspring, but each person is born with a will to direct his actions and seal his destiny, for which he alone is accountable before God.

Unlike other Judges, Samuel intended to create a legacy of leadership he could pass to his children. Samuel's corrupt perverse sons disappointed him and offended the nation. The Bible asserts that God took them at a young age. Samuel's dealings with Saul thereafter indicate that he harbored bitterness. He certainly bore guilt and shame. But Samuel learned valuable lessons that he was able to share and apply throughout his long life.

Disgruntled with the new king, Samuel set out to find a replacement.

This time he was providentially led to visit Bethlehem in the land of Judah where he called upon Jesse, the prominent grandson of Boaz and Ruth. Jesse's family now oversaw the fields of Boaz. Samuel told Jesse he wanted to interview his sons for a special assignment. The proud father delightedly paraded seven very impressive young men before the renowned prophet. Samuel didn't see what he was searching for.

That evening Jesse revealed that his youngest son was in the field tending their sheep, but he was sure Samuel wouldn't be interested in him. Nonetheless, Samuel entreated Jesse to fetch David so he could look him over. The custom in the day dictated the eldest son attend his father and learn how to lead the clan. Younger sons did most of the menial tasks, and the youngest in a family got stuck with the hardest dirtiest jobs that no one wanted to do. David routinely stayed with the sheep all night. He played his stringed instrument and sang songs he composed to draw them near and keep them calm.

He also had to run off or kill predators with his sling shot. Over the years David likely spent much time practicing and honing his skill. At slinging contests in Scotland and elsewhere over the past century expert hurlers have exhibited great precision. A good practitioner can launch a smooth stone at over 100 miles per hour and hit a small target repeatedly from thirty feet away.

When Samuel met David he exclaimed that David had what God was looking for to lead his people. "Men look on outward appearances, but God looks straight to the heart," he declared. Samuel anointed David with oil and prophesied that he would one day rule the nation of Israel.

Later, young David remained at home with the sheep when Saul drafted his older brothers to fight the army of the Philistines as Samuel had predicted years before. They were encamped at the Valley of Elah where neither side would cross the stream to attack. Instead, they taunted each other from a distance. Each army wanted the advantage of higher ground. The stalemate lasted for weeks.

Jesse sent David to the battleground with food and supplies for his sons and some of the other men. When David arrived he beheld a Philistine who was over nine feet tall standing at the stream harassing the Jews. He dared them to send out their best fighting man to meet him in hand to hand combat. "If I kill him, you will surrender and become our slaves," he proposed. "If he kills me, the Philistines will be your slaves." It was a simple proposition, but not a single Jew stepped forward. Goliath called out to them over and over, calling them women, and little boys, and cowards. He mocked them and made fun of their impotent God. Saul was humiliated as the crowd on the other side of the stream laughed and cursed at his army and his God.

David left the rations with his brothers and approached Saul. No one took him seriously when he volunteered to face the giant warrior. But David was serious and he persisted. Saul, with his nation at stake, allowed David to fight Goliath. He put the fate of Israel in a young shepherd boy's hands. The episode makes little sense at first glance, but thousands were there and the story circulated while David was a very public figure, and for centuries afterward. No one in Israel ever questioned it.

In modern culture we view David as the underdog that day. But that probably wasn't the case. No soldier in Israel's army could have beaten Goliath in a conventional match. David refused the customary shield, helmet, and armor that would confine him and weigh him down. He refused the king's sword or his armor bearer's heavy spear. God in his providence had placed David in a lonely field where he routinely prayed, sang hymns and composed poems to God by day and by night. David honed his slinging skills for hours on end. He was calm, confident and capable. He was born and groomed for such a time as this. When David firmly assured Saul, "God will give me this giant who mocks him," the king was apparently convinced.

Goliath lumbered under the weight of his great armor, shield and weapons. He had to get close to fell David. But David darted back and forth, nimble and energetic. Exhausted and exasperated, the giant let down his guard for more smack talk. David packed a single smooth round stone in his sling from thirty feet away, and grinned. The rest is legend, and history.

To this day, the Israeli army comfortably contends against great odds by playing to their own strengths, utilizing unique and superior resources, maintaining discipline in their ranks, honing and perfecting their skills, expecting to prevail, and relying on their God to deliver oppressive giants to them in battle.

26

A Great Kingdom

David became a national hero for killing Goliath. Not yet aware that Samuel anointed David to succeed him, Saul rewarded David by making him a military commander and bringing him into his trusted entourage. He recruited David into the royal family by arranging for him to marry one of his daughters.

Between Samuel's private and public beratings and the awesome burden of being Israel's first king, Saul grew anxious and paranoid. When he couldn't relax he called for David to lull him to sleep with psalms, or hymns, like the ones he improvised for his father's sheep. Saul grew to love David as he loved his own son, Jonathan. But he also grew apprehensive when he learned about David's relationship with Samuel.

Over time, Saul became obsessed with David, whom the people revered. Their relationship soured. Saul plotted to have David assassinated, but David remained loyal to the king. David was forced to flee and a small band followed him into the mountains southwest of Saul's capital at Gibeah, a few miles outside the present site of Jerusalem.

They dwelt in caves, coexisting with Philistines who still occupied the land between the mountains and the Mediterranean Sea south of the capital city and west of the Dead Sea.

Centuries later when Rome conquered Syria, Lebanon and Jordan they called the entire region their Syrian province. Later they conquered the land of the Philistines, referred to by Romans as Palestine. Still later Rome absorbed Israel into their Palestinian province. The current territorial disputes that plague the region date back to early border skirmishes between the Philistines whose capital of Gath was south of Gaza, and Jews whose capital of Gibeah was near Jerusalem. There were Jews living among the Philistines, and Philistines living among the Jews. The similarities that extend over three thousand years are uncanny.

David knew he had been anointed to be king of Israel, but he refused to raise his hand against Saul and left the matter, and the timing, in God's hands. When the Philistines, who had grown more bold and fierce, crossed into Israel's borders marching north and east, Saul met them at Mount Gilboah. He and his sons were killed and Israel was left in defenseless disarray.

Saul's only surviving son, Ishbaal, was anointed king, but only the northern tribes supported him. Under his reign the Hebrews ceded more land to the advancing Philistines. Abner, Saul's longstanding general, abandoned Ishbaal out of frustration and joined with the tribes of Judah and Benjamin who cast their lot with David. Ishbaal continued to lose ground until his own court assassinated him and threw their support behind David. In 1010 BC David assimilated the opposing tribes of Israel, and thus began a glorious kingdom that was constituted of power, peace and prosperity.

Instead of attacking the Philistines within his borders, David focused his attention on the Jebusites in their fortress on Mount Zion along the perimeter of ancient Urushalom. The city had a rich Semite history and was strategically located in neutral territory between Israel's northern and southern tribes. Foreboding terrain protected the city on three sides so advancing armies always attacked from the northwest. Thus, it was easy to defend.

David seized his objective by stealth, with almost no bloodshed. When the Philistines realized David intended to anchor the kingdom of Israel in Jerusalem they attacked viciously. David not only repelled their attacks, he handily defeated them and pushed them back to their original borders along the Mediterranean coastline.

Calling his people to remember God's promise to Abraham, Isaac, and Jacob, David extended the borders of Israel and prospered to become the unrivaled dominant influence in the Levant. In order to strengthen his kingdom, David adopted the local practice of taking wives and making allegiances with neighboring tribes and rival states. Contention grew among his ambitious sons, who were agitated by their conniving mothers. Rebellion was rampant.

Like Adam and Eve, Abraham and Sarah, and households today, the house of David began to crumble when self-determination prevailed over a commitment to find and serve the intent of the master creator. David, now embedded in his material enterprises, sought to repent and recalibrate, but like any object that has been stretched, torn, or broken, resuming and maintaining an original form or course became increasingly difficult. A great king referred to in the Bible as "a man after God's own heart," battled the proud sinful nature that was rooted in his humanity.

27

A Coming Kingdom

David was a brilliant reflection of the nation state of Israel. The Hebrews were by nature and by their upbringing a disciplined and constructive people. They lived among races that were predominantly unbridled and destructive. Abraham dug wells in the land of Canaan. Rival bands stole them or destroyed them. Jacob's clan developed the land of Goshen into the envy of Egyptians who enslaved them and compelled them to build and maintain their cities. Joshua assigned clear lasting manageable borders for the twelve tribal clans of Israel when they reoccupied Canaan. Those whom they displaced continued to raid and plunder each other and failed to recognize and honor each other's borders.

David contended for territory that had belonged to his forefathers and improved the property he occupied. Israel's adversaries all around conquered villages and left them in ruins. David purposefully amassed what hostile neighbors sought to take or destroy. Strong and determined, King David staved off his antagonists to build and adorn a splendid city for a proud nation in the midst of hooligans.

In modern Israel today, when missiles are launched, weapons are fired, or bombs explode, resilient industrious Jews are quick to repair and rebuild, while their counterparts seem content to live in rubble. One group has a mindset to build and preserve. The other posits that reparation is futile, improvement is a waste of time and effort, or worse, taking or retaking what others build or repair is more desirous than doing the hard and tedious work themselves.

As in any prospering enterprise in our time, David, the chief executive, grew comfortable in his role. He went out to battle with his troops and everyone realized he was no longer the young warrior he once was. When he was almost killed, his officers convinced him to stay in the palace and let them handle the wars. Bored and sleepless, he ventured onto the palace roof to survey his surroundings, what was already being called the splendid City of David. While there, he observed a beautiful woman bathing at a nearby house that belonged to one of his junior officers. He invited the young woman to his palace, romanced her, seduced her, and got her pregnant.

To cover up his affair with Bathsheba, David called her husband home under the guise of getting an update from the battlefront. After a brief meeting the king sent his valiant soldier home to spend time with his wife, but instead Uriah slept on David's porch with the palace guards, saying, "My leaders and those I respect are sleeping in tents and risking their lives for our great nation. How can I exercise my privilege and enjoy my wife?"

Clearly Uriah was a good soldier and a noble man. David was insistent and compelled him to stay another night only to find that he did the same thing. David sent Uriah back to the battle with a note instructing his commander to send him into the most violent fight and abandon him there. Upon confirming his death, David married his widow. The baby died, but Bathsheba had other sons for King David. Solomon followed his father David's reign and produced the ancestry of Joseph, a carpenter from Nazareth. Nathan's lineage produced Eli, the father of Mary the mother of Jesus Christ. These lineages provided the necessary credentials to establish Jesus as a prospective king over the nation of Israel a thousand years later.

Other sons by other wives and mistresses fell out of favor for various reasons, but David's clear favorite was Absalom, born to his wife Maacah while David was leader of Judah, before he was king over all Israel. The Bible indicates that Absalom was a near perfect physical specimen, and he was brilliant. As an adult he fomented a rebellion from his father's former base in Hebron. The coup temporarily unseated his father and was narrowly defeated. When David learned of his son's death he cried, "Oh my son Absalom, my son, my son Absalom! Would that I had died in your stead!"

David wrote the third Psalm when he fled from Absalom. He wrote many other songs in times of triumph, tragedy, celebration or frustration. To fully appreciate the 150 psalms contained in the Bible it helps to know their authors and understand where, when, and why they were written. Though they are gathered into one book, they were written over many years by several authors in various contexts.

By the end of his reign David was mature, mellow, and fully devoted to God. Israel was unified and prosperous. David's overriding remaining objective was to build a magnificent shrine to God. He called the priests together and assigned roles. From that time only direct descendants of Moses' brother Aaron would oversee worship. The rest of the Levi family tribe became scribes and Temple servants.

David appointed Zadok as High Priest because he was the head of the household of Eleazar, Aaron's son and successor. The Zadokites of David's time ultimately became Zadocees or Sadducees, the materialistic establishment priests of Jesus' time. For centuries, only descendants of Zadok were recognized as heads of the priesthood, suitable for the office of High Priest. Aaron's lineage would produce the Levitical priest who begot Elizabeth, the mother of John the Baptist and aunt of Jesus Christ. John's father, the great priest Zachariah, was a descendant of Abijah who oversaw the eighth turn of service in the Tabernacle at Jerusalem for King David.

28

A Prosperous Kingdom

Like his father before him, King Solomon was devoted to the God of Israel. His chief preoccupation was establishing a suitable place for God to dwell among his people. David's shrine to God was an elaborate tent. Solomon built a genuine Temple, a more permanent structure. It took seven years to build it and thirteen more to build the complex around it.

Assuming the throne in his youth, Solomon's dying father told him he would have to grow up fast. Solomon prayed that God would give him a righteous understanding mind to discern between good and evil in order that he might be able to govern God's people. His wisdom was illustrated in the account of two women who both claimed an infant was theirs.

The women were brought before the new king to resolve the matter. To quickly get to the bottom of the issue Solomon asked for a sword and proposed to cut the child in half and divide him between them. One of the women flippantly observed that neither half would be of any value, but the other collapsed and screamed, "No! No! Give the child to her." Solomon knew at once which one was the child's birth mother.

Solomon created twelve taxing districts that overlapped traditional borders in order to diffuse tribal allegiance and consolidate power in Jerusalem. He then pacified clan leaders by following in his father's footsteps and marrying women from every tribe or state. He also married women from outside Israel's borders to assure peace with their neighbors. One of Solomon's brides was the daughter of Pharaoh Siamun of the 21st dynasty. In centuries past, the Pharaohs married the daughters of foreign potentates. Now a Pharaoh gave a princess of Egypt to the king of Israel, a significant change in protocol. Egypt was waning and Israel was rising.

Israel enjoyed unprecedented prosperity during Solomon's reign, in part because the entire Levant was experiencing strong economic growth. Trade replaced warfare among the nations and Jews proved to be superior entrepreneurs and traders. Wealthy nations were attracted to Israel and were awestruck by Solomon. Israel contracted for the best wood, the best fabrics, and the most precious metals from far away nations that were pleased to supply it at bargain prices, or provided it for the honor of doing business with Solomon. Only the best materials, and the best foreign workmen, were used to build Solomon's great Temple to the God of Israel.

Tamrin, an Ethiopian wood merchant, returned to advise his queen about the splendor of Israel and the greatness of her king. Makeda, the beautiful and sophisticated queen of Sheba traveled for months over mountains and deserts to bring camel loads of East African gold and fine spices like frankincense and myrrh to Jerusalem. Both leaders were highly intelligent and comely and bonded over sharing riddles late into the night. Makeda converted to Judaism during her visit. History indicates she had a son named Malida, from whom the Ethiopian dynasty claims to descend to the present day, by her union with Solomon. Makeda reigned over Ethiopian territory, including

Yemen across the strait, for fifty years. Today the magistrate of Ethiopia still bears the mantra, "Lion of Judah".

When Solomon began to build a temple for God in earnest, citizens of Israel contributed gifts in excess of $100 million in today's currency beyond their obligatory tithes and taxes. Solomon also established fortified cities like Gezer, Hazor, and Megiddo to protect his kingdom. Several of those cities have been excavated in the last century.

Although Solomon was devoted to God, the older he got the more permissive he got, allowing his many wives to openly worship and promote their various gods. Though prophets scolded him and admonished him otherwise, Solomon tolerated the idolatry that led to compromise, perversion, and ultimately sacrilege. As diversity spread, people adopted politically correct attitudes and morality decayed. The nation lost its focus and its vitality. The weight of Solomon's opulent lifestyle coupled with a downturn in economic activity ushered in higher taxes that produced diminishing returns. Selfish inattentive leadership led to decline. By the end of Solomon's reign, his government was fractured and starting to degenerate. A once very wise man behaved foolishly when he abandoned godly pursuits.

Samuel warned Israel about kingdoms. They follow a natural course. Man was designed to be individually accountable to God. Men can govern or steward, but God must ultimately rule. Creative willful people, given free rein in paradise, eventually choose to gratify themselves. Worldly leaders are inclined to impose their will and place blame when things don't work out. Moral failings always lead to spiritual brokenness that leads to decay and results in death. When the blind follow the blind, they both end up in a ditch.

Solomon led a prosperous nation into decay. But every individual was responsible for his state of being. Every citizen of the world faces the same dilemma, now as then. Whether in a garden, a city, or wherever you find yourself, "men look on outward appearances, but God looks straight to the heart." We are made to reflect the image of "I am" regardless of our earthly citizenship. God is to reign over our character regardless of worldly leaders who impose their will over us. The bar is higher and the stakes are raised for those who find themselves in a position to impose their will on others.

29

A Divided Kingdom

Upon Solomon's death around 930 BC, his forty one year old son, Rehoboam, assumed the throne. The district counselors called for a meeting at Shechem where they gave Rehoboam a list of grievances and demanded tax relief. The new king was advised by his father's courtiers that he should acknowledge their complaints and entertain their reasonable requests, but instead Rehoboam listened to the young elite scholars he brought into his administration. Out of touch with the common folk who were the backbone of the nation, they recommended that Rehoboam crack down hard and show them he was in charge now. It backfired. The tribes revolted. They stoned Adoniram, the court official in charge of levying taxes, and chased the king and his military escort back to Jerusalem.

The rebel leaders cried, "What portion do we have in David's inheritance? Let the house of David fend for itself and let every man of Israel go back to his own tent." They formed a confederation of states and called on Jeroboam from the tribe of Ephraim to be their leader. Solomon had appointed Jeroboam to oversee the labor forces that worked on building the great Temple. Ironically, he was accused of plotting a mutiny and fled to Egypt before being called back to lead the northern tribes of Israel.

David, Solomon, and Rehoboam were from the tribe of Judah. Judah was the fourth son of Israel and the one whom Jacob passed his scepter to, saying that someone from the clan of Judah would reign over isra El forever. Jeroboam was a descendant of Ephraim, the son of Judah's brother Joseph. For centuries the rivalry between Judah and Ephraim had been bitter and intense. Rehoboam came to rule over Judah and that portion of Benjamin where the district line had been drawn. The southern kingdom retained their capital in Jerusalem and with it, the great Temple. The rest of Israel, now so called, kept their tribal borders and made Shechem, where Simeon and Levi avenged Dinah, their northern capital.

The Valley of Shechem was considered sacred to the Jews. It's where Abraham built his first altar, Isaac pitched his tent with Rebekah, and Jacob dug his famous well. The cave tomb of Joseph near the site where he was once sold to slave-traders was still undisturbed. Here, between Mt Ebal and Mt Gerizim, Joshua etched the laws of Moses in a prism stone.

In order to differentiate themselves from the southern kingdom, Jeroboam dismissed the Levites from their priestly duties among the other tribes and revived the ancient altars at Bethel and Dan. Priests were selected from among the common ranks. Soon pagan worship crept back into the mainstream. Israel faltered morally, but thrived economically under Omri, the sixth king of the northern tribes. He built a new capital southwest of Shechem and called it Samaria. His son Ahab finished building their elaborate temple, parts of which can be seen today.

Ahab married Jezebel, a Phoenician queen, and enjoyed an influx of funds with which he constructed a magnificent altar to her god, Baal. Jezebel imported hundreds of priests to administer her temple as weak

Hebrew practitioners dared not object until a prophet named Elijah arose from Gilead, east of the Jordan River. Out of nowhere Elijah approached Ahab condemning his rule and pronouncing a drought on the land. Before Ahab could have him arrested, Elijah vanished into the desert. It didn't rain for the next three years.

Elijah returned and issued a public challenge to his adversaries. They met at Mount Carmel where the priests of Baal cut wood and built a huge pyre. They killed a bull and hoisted it atop the stacked wood. Then they danced and sang and prayed. Elijah chided, "Scream louder, maybe your god is hard of hearing. Perhaps he's gone away on a journey. Or, maybe he's sleeping and you need to wake him up." The priests of Baal cut themselves with knives and burned themselves with fire in their self-effacing worship. They chanted and pled with Baal to consume their offering, but they couldn't keep a fire lit.

Elijah quietly shook his head, cut wood, and prayed. He killed a bull to match the pagan offering and prayed again. Then, curiously, he doused his altar with well water making it virtually impossible to light a fire. When he stepped aside to pray again, a bolt of lightning consumed the bull and set his pyre ablaze. Thousands of people who came out to celebrate and witness the contest dropped to their knees. "How long will you limp along tripping over two opposing courses?" Elijah posed to the crowd. "If Baal is your choice, then follow him. But if God is your choice, then follow God!" The people seized and killed every prophet of Baal. Rain poured from heaven. The drought ended.

Elijah remains the outstanding prophet of Israel. He performed many recorded miracles. He forecasted hundreds of events, all of which happened or remained pending until they happened hundreds of years later as foretold. None of Elijah's prophecies proved vain or false. He restored traditional worship in Israel, then he personally selected and mentored Elisha as his successor.

Meanwhile in the southern kingdom, Rehoboam, who followed the unwise counsel of his young elite friends and led Judah into idolatry, repented when he realized he was under siege because he sapped the moral strength of his nation. When the nation turned back to following the God of their heritage they were able to repel their enemies. They reformed and began to rebuild.

Rehoboam's son Abijah succeeded him. Like his father, Abijah followed God but wasn't fully committed. He sustained the nation, but they didn't prosper. Abijah's son Asa on the other hand was devoted to God. Rehoboam began the process of tearing down pagan temples in Judah. Abijah continued to dismantle and retract the compromises and politically correct concessions that weakened the country, but Asa was zealous and actively sought genuine godly reform.

Azariah prophesied, "The Lord is with those who are with him. Those who seek him, find him. But if you disregard him, he will disregard you. Stay on track and you will be rewarded." Devout Israelites from Ephraim, Manasseh, Simeon and surrounding tribes left floundering Israel and joined with Asa. Judah started prospering again. Nineteen kings reigned over the northern kingdom of Israel in a span of almost 200 years. Twelve kings reigned in Judah during the same period, and Judah survived another 140 years under eight more rulers. Some were good, some were bad, on both sides of the border.

30

Kings and Prophets

Though they shared a lineage and remained close allies, Judah and Israel became increasingly distinct with the passage of time and changes in leadership. While the northern kingdom of Israel suffered under the rule of Ahab, King Asa died in Judah and his son Jehoshaphat ascended to the throne in the southern kingdom.

Jehoshaphat was a righteous man and a good king who was determined to purge idolatry and restore ethical leadership. He assumed the crown of Judah when he was thirty five and lived to be sixty. Jehoshaphat saw what was happening in Israel and cast out prophets of Baal and Ashtoreth, though the citizens of Judah no longer seemed to share his devotion to the God of his great grandfather, King David.

Jehoshaphat restored Judah's military prowess and drafted a peace treaty and a trade pact with his cousins in Israel. He sent priests from Jerusalem out to the towns and villages of Judah introducing an early form of rabbinical teaching. Judah prospered under Jehoshaphat's rule and he became very wealthy. Faith in God was restored in the southern kingdom.

In the north, dozens of Arab tribal leaders joined forces with the King of Syria to come against King Ahaziah in Samaria, now the capital of Israel. They demanded that Ahaziah turn over the national treasury and surrender his wives and children. Ahaziah reluctantly conceded, expecting his Arab enemies to turn back and spare the rest of his nation. However, when the aggressors assessed that Ahaziah was weak and not inclined to fight back, they increased their demands. They said they intended to plunder the city and make Israel a vassal state, and they would take whoever and whatever they wanted back with them.

Following Judah's lead into repentance, Israel stood their ground. Instead of waiting to be overrun, the citizens of Israel united in appealing to God in prayer. Then they attacked and handily defeated their foes. Israel enjoyed peace for three years while Syria rebuilt their army only to try again. This time an even larger stronger force invaded, taking possession of Ramoth Gilead. The people of Israel rallied to counterattack and again enjoyed a surprising victory. But the Jews spared the life of the wicked enemy king who provoked his followers to shun God and resist Israel's religious influence. Through the ensuing decades Syria remained one of Israel's many nemeses, as it is to this day.

Far to the south, Edomites who descended from Esau dwelled along the southern border of Judah. Esau was Jacob's older brother from whom he supplanted, or stole, the family birthright their father Isaac inherited from Abraham. Esau made a truce and moved south, ceding the better land to Jacob when he came back from Haran. When the Jews returned from their years of captivity in Egypt, Esau's clan controlled the famous King's Highway as it passed through Edom. They forbade passage to the Jews and forced them around and over the mountains.

The Jews tolerated Edomites because they were close cousins. The Edomites didn't initiate attacks against Judah, but they always helped and supported other nations that did. Obadiah prophesied, "Because you provoke the people of your brother, you will be covered with shame and destroyed forever. When you stood aloof while strangers confiscated their wealth and foreigners invaded and contended for Jerusalem, you were as bad as them. The house of Jacob will cling to its inheritance. But no one will survive from the house of Esau." Throughout their history the Edomites begrudged the Jews.

During the Maccabean wars of the first century BC the Edomites, ancestors of Esau who were by then known as Idumaeans, the Greek language equivalent, were conquered and absorbed into Judah. The Roman Empire emerged and Caesar selected as his surrogate Judean king a compliant Idumaean whose father had converted to Judaism out of expedience. That Idumaean is known in history as King Herod the Great, the tyrant who ordered a massacre in Bethlehem in an attempt to kill the Christ. His son, Herod Antipas, later conspired with the Jewish High Priest, Caiaphas, to have Jesus tried before Pilate. After the Herod clan died off, Idumaeans slowly disappeared in accordance with Obadiah's prophecy that Edom would perish. Today the race is lost to history.

Every person on Earth has a material body with a brain that guides a will. God is a spirit, and we are made in his image. We are physical and we are spiritual. Some people allow their spirituality to dominate their outlook on life. Others maintain a more materialistic worldview. For those who are more spiritual, morality is guided by faith. For those who are more materialistic, morality is guided by logic. Faith and logic are both terms for what a person honestly believes and relies on.

Herod, the offspring of Esau, exemplified a logical selfish morality. Jesus, a descendant of Esau's twin brother Jacob, who became Israel, came to exemplify a faith-based God-honoring selfless morality. The opposing worldviews cannot coexist without compromising fundamental tenets, and one or the other will grow to dominate every individual. One or the other will prevail. The Bible submits that in the end truth will emerge and unveil all human error and deception.

31

Jonah's Rough Journey

In light of today's news broadcasts it isn't hard to imagine a large metropolis where murder, rape, and robbery were commonplace and poverty and unemployment were almost universal. No one cleaned cluttered streets. Women and girls didn't venture alone in public, even in daylight. They exposed no flesh and looked into no man's eyes. Schools closed and plundered markets stood empty and vacant.

Gangs of men and boys routinely raided nearby districts, abducted children, destroyed property, took what they wanted, and killed anyone who stood in their way. There was no municipal policing and the totalitarian government was impenetrably corrupt. Rules of conduct were based on a harsh religion that engaged in infant sacrifice and slave prostitution. Soldiers tortured civilians for entertainment and dissidents were publicly beheaded or burned in the streets.

While crowds gathered in courtyards and chanted "death to Jews", a frustrated rabbi in a once pleasant village no longer a safe distance away counseled yet another family whose child was missing. He closed his door, dropped to his knees, and pondered what could be done about the growing crisis. He prayed to God and begged for mercy. "God, destroy these filthy perverts. They're not fit to occupy your planet."

Every day his prayer was interrupted by the same nagging inspiration. "What? Me? No way!" he muttered aloud. But he couldn't shut out the voice in his head. Every time he looked into the terrified faces of his neighbors the voice drowned out their tearful pleas for consolation and protection. Around 780 BC God tapped a prophet named Jonah to confront the Assyrians in their perilous capital of Nineveh. Nineveh was much like Sodom and Gomorrah had been in Abraham's day, but larger and more violent. Jonah detested the Ninevites and called for their annihilation. Instead of confronting them, he chose to board a ship that was headed the opposite way.

The forces of nature opposed the ship such that it tossed and would have been destroyed. Everyone on board sought the intervention of whatever god he recognized. Meanwhile, Jonah slept through the storm. The superstitious crew casted lots to see who was to blame for their suffering and the lot fell to Jonah. "Who are you? What have you done to turn the gods against us?" they demanded.

Jonah identified himself as a Jewish priest who was rebelling against God's unction to do something he didn't want to do. "I am the source of your agony," he confessed. Disinterested bystanders who didn't even acknowledge God were clearly forced to suffer because of sin in their midst. One of the great lessons of Jonah is that no matter how complicated or theological one looks at the matter, sin always spills over into the world around us and innocent people have to suffer when any of us defies God.

Jonah compelled the anxious crew to throw him overboard in order to save themselves. Fearing for their lives, every member of the crew bowed and called upon Jonah's God, sought guidance and forgiveness, and ultimately did as Jonah suggested. Immediately upon ridding themselves of the rebellious spirit in their midst, the storm passed and the sea calmed. A second lesson is that when you sever your relationships with rebellious people, life assumes a calmer less dramatic course.

Jonah was consumed by a creature of the sea. The Bible doesn't say it was a whale, though it may have been mammalian to capture adequate oxygen to sustain Jonah for long periods underwater. The Bible only states it was in the sea and God created it. Clearly, God supernaturally directed its course. The creature swallowed Jonah whole and submerged completely. Jonah's condition was reasonably described as comatose, but he was for a time aware of his general surroundings. He prayed and repented, not expecting to live through the ordeal.

According to the Jewish reckoning of days, Jonah was in the "belly" of the creature for anywhere between 33 and 70 hours. On the third day he was expelled onto the shore several miles from Nineveh. Gastric fluids dissolved much of his hair and beard and ate at his skin. He must have looked like a man who survived a fire with first and second degree burns over his entire body. His garment was ripped and tattered. He was scary looking, tender and sensitive. And he stunk.

The sun hurt. The wind hurt. Walking and moving hurt. Yet he made a vow and now he would honor it. He marched into Nineveh preaching against their sin and calling them to repentance. Forty days in a row Jonah traversed a city whose breadth was a three day journey, drawing amazing crowds. At last, he scaled a hill overlooking the city. When he sat down under a vine, it mysteriously blossomed to give him shade and block the wind. Even as God miraculously shielded and comforted him, Jonah prayed to die, and called upon God to rain fire on Nineveh to destroy the wicked pagans. To his amazement, the people of Nineveh responded to his message. They turned from evil and sought God.

Rather than being thrilled or relieved, Jonah was disgusted. Like a modern Christian or Jew walking into a bastion of Islamic State terrorists who brutally plundered his village and killed his family, Jonah didn't want to go, didn't expect them to listen, and didn't care if God spared them. His response was totally understandable. However, God was not reinforcing logic, but faith; another great lesson of Jonah.

Jonah's story is acceptable as it stands, according to how much faith a person has in what his God is able to do in the nature He created and sustains. The people of Jonah's day took it at face value. Seven hundred years later, Jesus mentioned it not as allegorical, but as emblematic of his time in a grave from which he would arise.

Miracles are phenomena that defy the natural order. This miracle is threefold. First, Jonah was preserved and his very life is a testimony of God's mercy on a defiant soul. Second, the vile people of Nineveh exhibited wholesale repentance. A huge secular community altered its course by accepting a spiritually dominated worldview. And third, it was a prophetic foreshadowing of another event that followed hundreds of years later. Acceptance of that event is the singular benchmark of modern orthodox Christianity where life is more than a temporal physical manifestation.

Part 5

Fall and Restoration

32

Fall of the Northern Kingdom

In the days of Abraham, Isaac, and Jacob, Assyria was composed of parts of modern Syria, Turkey, Iran and Iraq. It's the area east of Eden that Cain was banished to after he slew his brother Able. The term Assyria is derived from Ashuria. The Hebrew letter shin has an "s" sound and a "sh" sound. Ashur and his nephew Nimrod built cities where Hamites settled soon after the flood of Noah's era.

Assyrians were worldly and sophisticated. They were the first to pave roads, use kilns to make pottery, and make weapons and armor out of iron. They adopted cuneiform writing from the Sumerians and were the first to build libraries. They had a postal system that routinely shuttled messages and correspondence between at least five major cities. They utilized aqueducts and indoor plumbing.

The prophet Jonah preached at Nineveh, the Assyrian capital, which lies ninety feet below ground near modern Mosul in Iraq. Assyrians tried to blot God out of their society and plugged in gods of their own making. Impacted by Jonah's proclamation, they experienced great revival. A few decades later they were again renowned as the most brutal of civilizations, a testament to humanity's secular inclination.

The Assyrians swept through the Levant when Israel and Judah were weak. When the prophet Joel called the Jews back to their roots they restored the Temple and made some gains. However, Joel was frustrated because their culture remained materialistic and corruption was imbedded in their leadership ranks. Over time, Israel and Judah succumbed to the dominant influence of the Assyrians.

Hosea, a contemporary of Joel, was compelled to prophesy Israel's fate through his marriage to a prostitute named Gomer. Hosea genuinely loved Gomer, but she was drawn to other lovers. They had three children. Jezreel was so named because it meant "estranged from God". Luruhamah meant "no respect". And Loammi signified ultimate rejection because it meant "not mine".

Hosea viewed his marriage to Gomer as an irrevocable commitment. Time and again, he found her when she strayed, fought for her freedom, bought her out of bondage, coveted her when she was unworthy, and forgave her when she was unfaithful. He railed against Israel, calling them to repentance out of personal experience. He warned that God was running out of patience with a partner that stubbornly refused to remain committed and faithful.

The people praised Amos, another contemporary prophet, when he spoke out against the wickedness of the Syrians, Philistines, Edomites, Ammonites and Moabites. They applauded the pending downfall of others, but when he turned his attention to Israel their countenance fell. Amos testified that God established the Jews as an example, but they faltered and lost credibility among neighboring clans. An immerging power, the Assyrians, would soon trample the lot of them. Logic indicates people should be able to succeed if they follow those who prosper in the world. But prudence dictates that men must conform to God. Over and over, the prophets warned the stubborn masses who were too self-absorbed to heed.

Successive prophets warned the people of God that they would soon become alienated. Their cries would go unheeded. God allows every person to believe and act as he wants, but reality ultimately prevails. Israel chose her course and God would no longer stand in her way. The chosen race better reflected the image of worldliness than people of godliness. Amos' last words to Israel's king were, "Israel will surely go into exile, away from their native land." Within a decade of Amos' pronouncement Tiglath-Pileser, otherwise known in history as King Pul, began extracting Israelites to serve him as slaves in Assyria. By 722 BC the nation of Israel was plundered. All the smug people of Israel were taken to Nineveh as slaves, and scattered to various cities and camps.

Micah, Amos' contemporary, saw and foretold the imminent fall of Israel and followed up with a warning for Judah. The basis of the prophets' rebukes was corporate sin evidenced by rampant greed, corruption, and idol worship. The people who "belonged to God" were no longer "devoted to God". When an item is no longer fit for its purpose and cannot be repaired it gets discarded by its disappointed frustrated owner.

Though the prophets preached doom and gloom, they also held out the prospect of redemption. God would not abandon his people. God never forsakes what is rightfully his. He merely stops contending with that which remains defiant and unruly. He lets the nature he created run its course, and patiently waits to reward those who are willing to invite him back into their lives on his terms.

God's people prospered when they subjected themselves to his authority in pursuit of his purposes. The message of the prophets could be boiled down to, "You're certainly free to live for yourself with reckless abandon, and reap whatever you sow. However, if you prefer what God has in store, discipline and apply yourself to his pursuits and grooming. It's totally up to you."

Many prophecies in Israel and Judah concerned a Messiah, or savior. Messiah would be a human champion who would arise from among

God's people to unite them and lead them back into right standing in relation to God. Many messianic prophecies were very specific relating to his birthplace, his temperament, his phenomenal achievements, and his ascension to power only to be rejected by the ruling secular elite. Even his mode of death was foretold, though it did not yet exist.

When Judah declined to align with Syria and Israel to contend for local territory against the Assyrians, Syria and Israel joined forces and turned on Judah only to foolishly weaken all three. Isaiah prophesied that Israel and Syria would soon fall, and they did. Isaiah went on to record hundreds of spectacular judgments and predictions that unfolded over the ensuing centuries. What he said about individual leaders, nations, clans, and even unknown distant future events is startling in its accuracy. Israel fell because her leaders and her people failed to heed the prophets' warnings and determined to apply human logic instead of seeking guidance and direction from the object of their faith. Looking back, we perceive they should have known better. Yet, we follow their course.

33

Reprieve for Judah

To stave off the Assyrians who took their cousins in Israel captive, King Hezekiah of Judah raided the sacred Temple in Jerusalem and turned over the abundant gold and silver it contained. Then he agreed to tax his people and make tribute payments to the Assyrian king. Convinced there was more loot to come, and that tiny Judah was a manageable province, the Assyrian army backed off.

Isaiah, the popular widely revered prophet, advised several kings before Hezekiah ascended. He encouraged Hezekiah to lead the nation to repent, and noting Israel's demise, Hezekiah destroyed the idolatrous shrines his predecessors had built. Isaiah was pleased with Hezekiah's religious zeal, but Hezekiah disregarded Isaiah's political counsel and like Solomon's son, Rehoboam, listened to the aristocratic scholars and politicians that surrounded him.

Hezekiah made a pact with Egypt, their neighbor to the south with whom they had exchanged royal brides. Hezekiah diverted funds he collected for the Assyrians into the Egyptian treasury in exchange for their promise of support if Judah was invaded and war broke out.

The prophets shook their heads in disgust. No feeble worldly power could protect and preserve a nation in crisis, only God can do that. Hezekiah turned to worldly resources in lieu of his better unseen option. Then as now, it was a poor choice. Egypt took more from Judah than they were ever able to provide. That is the way of the world.

War was inevitable so Hezekiah fortified Jerusalem and bolstered the walls. He restored a shaft that had been burrowed through the mountain to the spring of Gihon that provided water to the city. He finished his project and anxiously waited. Isaiah warned him that an attack was immanent and, as always, he was right. King Sennacherib, himself, led a powerful invasion force. In his prism stone, now on display in the British Museum, he boasted he laid siege to 46 of Judah's strong cities. One of the panels depicts a tower on wheels battering the walls of Jerusalem. Another panel shows impaled Jewish warriors being hung on stakes by Assyrian soldiers while tearful women and children stood by and grieved.

Driven to his knees, Hezekiah turned to Isaiah for advice. Isaiah calmly told him to wait on the Lord and do nothing rash. "Take heed. Don't get ruffled, and don't be faint of heart. As he came, so he will depart. The alien king will not enter this city." Sennacherib's siege was mysteriously lifted when a terrible disease that didn't affect the Jews rapidly spread among his troops. Over a hundred thousand of his soldiers died according to Sennacherib's own records. The Assyrians retreated back to Nineveh, but Judah lay in ruins. Though Hezekiah boasted he did not submit to Sennacherib, his battered country remained under Assyrian domination.

Over the next few decades under a foreign yoke, alien influences lured Judah back into pagan practices as they became more politically correct. King Jehoiakim grew culturally lax and allowed a shrine to be erected for the worshippers of Moloch in Jerusalem. That eventually led to children being sacrificed as was the custom at other foreign altars. Mutilated little bodies were tossed over the cliff into the Valley of the sons of Hinnom, later known as Gehenna. The Bible credits that atrocity, above all others, for the ultimate doom of the nation of Judah. Genuine modern pro-life advocates fear the same national fate.

When a righteous Jew named Uriah rose up and railed against Moloch and other foreign cults, King Jehoiakim, claiming to be sophisticated and open-minded, had him put to death for his "over-zealous religious hate crime". That gave rise to Jeremiah, the son of a very popular priest from Anathoth, three miles north of Jerusalem. Jeremiah went to the Temple in Jerusalem and proclaimed repentance or doom for Judah. He reminded his audience that God did not punish the sins of his people, as was and is the common notion, but judged them according to their sin, or degree of alienation from him. Abominable acts are but the result of, and evidence of, alienation from God.

The Jewish concept of repentance is different from our modern understanding. Christian preachers use the Greek term, metanoia, to invoke people to "change their direction" or "turn from their wicked ways." That is partially correct. The Hebrew term, toshuveh, actually refers to calibration. By recalibrating our orientation to focus on God, we shed diversions and distractions that draw us to ungodly thoughts and actions. It's not simply a matter of changing the channel, but getting on a singular correct frequency without the interference of other channels.

Jeremiah proposed the only command God ever really gave anyone was, "Obey my voice and I will be your God, and you can be my people." Jehoiakim, a secular governor, observed and tolerated the notion there might be powerful spiritual forces operating in the world, but rejected the idea that a man should subvert his will and actually live his life serving a nebulous higher power. Jehoiakim had Jeremiah beaten and put in stocks overnight. He only released him fearing the outcry of the masses. Forbidden to enter the Temple precinct again, Jeremiah directed his devoted scribe, Baruch, to preach on his behalf.

Through the ages, those who haven't liked God's consistent message have sought to silence or kill brave noble messengers. True prophets never said, "Listen to me." Under scrutiny, they always decreed, "Seek God, and always do as he leads you to do." The Bible's theme echoes that every person is designed to submit to spiritual guidance on a material journey through a physical world. Each of us is independently accountable to God for our actions and reactions.

34

Fall of the Southern Kingdom

Manasseh was perhaps the most despicable king in Judah's history. His son Amon assumed the throne and lasted only two years. Then Josiah ascended when he was only eight years old and turned out to be one of Judah's finest kings. The course of a Nation can turn quickly under good, or bad, leadership. Josiah took counsel from his uncle, Zephaniah, a righteous man of Josiah's royal lineage who rose up to become a prophet of God.

Josiah grew to be a great reformer. He was zealous for righteousness without being overly religious. He attacked with vengeance the pagan practices that had infiltrated Judah. He tore down temples and shrines and burned cult priests on their own altars. He so utterly destroyed the idols and articles of worship that they were unrecognizable. Then he had them burned and ground to powder and scattered them on their dead practitioners' graves.

Under Zephaniah's influence, Josiah did not seek to convert his people back to their Jewish religion and worship practices. He turned the people and their leaders back to God. Although many priests and prophets were groomed or educated by the religious elite, the most outstanding figures in the Bible were not. Zephaniah, like Isaiah, Elisha, Amos and many others, rose up reluctantly and spoke out boldly. Their zeal was in their bowels and they understood that wickedness was the true enemy.

Then, as now, true spiritual leadership was not vested in those who boasted of their moral superiority, but those who were contrite over their broken condition and deeply burdened for the lost and wayward souls of a nation gone astray. Faith is built on beliefs and conviction. Religion is composed of rituals and rules of conduct. Zephaniah and Josiah rightly observed that people didn't crave religion, as religious adherents often propose and promote. They simply needed to put their faith in a better source.

Upon turning the nation back to God, blessings and prosperity again flowed. But seeds of selfishness were buried deep and were broadly rooted in the culture. God admonished the people through his prophets, but every time the Jews were at the brink of total commitment they compromised. A weed, carelessly overlooked, will eventually take over a yard. A virus, not eradicated, will wreak havoc when unleashed. Evil, allowed to exist in the name of compassion, tolerance, or political correctness, always eventually comes back to kill or destroy future descendants of a family or a nation.

The Bible reveals that savage Assyrians took the Israelites hostage and removed them to camps in their homeland. Secular history adds that it was not uncommon for Assyrians to torture their captives by dipping them in boiling tar, or even skinning them alive. They raided villages and compelled residents to stay inside while their homes burned. Their conquests, their sports, and their politics were vicious and nasty. They menaced the nation of Judah for another century after they took Israel captive.

Jeremiah the prophet arose from obscurity at a young age warning of impending national peril at a time when dominant popular voices were spinning facts to disguise the unflattering truth. Leaders foolishly overstated the fragile peace and foundationless prosperity that surrounded them. Nahum prophesied the fall of Nineveh forty years before it happened and his vision was vivid and accurate. The huge city was so thoroughly destroyed that it took 2500 years for archeologists to stumble upon it. The city was considered a Bible myth until Sir Austen Layard began excavating it in the nineteenth century.

Political and religious leaders that represented the establishment of their day tried to dismiss or discredit prophets of God by labeling them crazy extremists. Jeremiah suffered constant ridicule, rejection and persecution over a fifty year span. But controversial prophets gained credibility when the masses deduced that they were accurate in their assessments and predictions, even concerning matters they could not have naturally foreseen.

Jeremiah foresaw the rise of a Babylonian empire long before it developed. He prophesied that Nineveh would eventually give way to a Medo-Persian alliance that didn't exist yet. In 605 BC Assyria, Babylonia, and Egypt clashed at Carchemish with King Nebuchadnezzar of Babylon emerging as the victor. The Babylonians became the dominant superpower in the world and King Nebuchadnezzar called all the regional kings, including Jehoiakim of Judah, to a summit at Babylonia in Babylon, better known today as Bagdad in Iraq. There, he forced all of them to agree to a heavy annual tribute. Jehoiakim started plotting a doomed rebellion as soon as he got home.

Jeremiah told Jehoiakim he didn't need to revolt, he simply needed to repent, but his words fell on deaf ears. Regardless of Jehoiakim's political zeal or military might, Jeremiah warned that if God's people did not repent, "the entire nation will fall into ruin and become a wasteland. And these remaining tribes of Israel will serve the king of Babylon for seventy years." In 598 BC Nebuchadnezzar fulfilled that prophecy when he marched to Jerusalem and toppled Jehoiakim's son, Jehoiachin, who succeeded him. The young king and his family were taken to Babylon, and Judah was crushed under even heavier taxes. Jehoiachin's uncle, Zedekiah, was put on the throne as Nebuchadnezzar's vassal. Nine years later, he too rebelled and kindled the wrath of his oppressors.

Nebuchadnezzar's powerful army breached the walls of Jerusalem in 586 BC, slaughtered thousands upon thousands of people, and utterly destroyed the sacred Temple. Jeremiah was spared and exiled to Egypt because Nebuchadnezzar heard of the prophet's efforts to restrain Jehoiakim, Jehoiachin and Zedekiah. But Judah, consisting of the last remnant of the tribal nations who descended from the family of Israel, was plundered.

The masses were dismissive, but the world was changing and God's prophets saw what lay in store. Even young King Josiah's reforms were not enough to stave off what the prophets saw as a nation's predictable fate based on abandoning their sovereign God. They waited too long, compromised too much, and drifted astray too many times to get one more last chance. That message from the prophets echoes over the annals of time to all those who still insist on charting their course while taunting God. ·

35

Deportation to Babylon

The Babylonians combed through Judah looking for the strongest, smartest, most physically attractive young men and women to serve as slaves. Refusing to go ensured death or mistreatment for captives and their family members.

Daniel, Hananaiah, Mishael and Azariah were among the first immigrants, along with the young prophet Ezekiel. The first four were assigned to serve in the king's court and given Babylonian names of Belteshazzar, Shadrach, Meshach, and Abednego. Ezekiel was sent to a refugee camp outside Tel-Abib to work on a canal between the Euphrates and Kebar rivers that irrigated farmland north of Babylonia.

Those who were to serve the king were put into a training and grooming regimen that ensured their health and success. Instead of violating prescribed Jewish dietary laws, Daniel persuaded the instructors to let them eat vegetables and drink only water. In a ten day trial, they not only survived, they excelled.

A few years went by and Nebuchadnezzar began having a recurring dream. When his counselors couldn't interpret its meaning he got so frustrated he had them put to death. One night Daniel dreamed the same dream and dared to step forward to interpret it for the king. In this dream Daniel saw a great statue arise from the earth with a head of gold. Next, its shoulders, arms, and chest of silver appeared. Its belly and thighs were made of bronze and its legs were iron. Then it stood on feet of clay.

A rock was hurled from heaven and crushed the feet of clay, causing the entire statue to tumble and fall apart. Dust blew in the wind and the heap became a mountain that spread to cover the entire land. Daniel explained that the golden head represented Nebuchadnezzar. The silver, iron, bronze and clay represented lesser kingdoms that would succeed the Babylonian empire. All those were swept away by a kingdom God would toss into the world to rule over people of all nations.

The king heaped honor and riches on Daniel for his interpretation and promoted him to a position in his government. Nebuchadnezzar then commissioned a huge golden statue to be cast in his own likeness and commanded that everyone should bow to his image. While Daniel was away on an errand of the king, another courtier reported that Daniel's three Jewish friends would not bow to the statue, but bowed to worship their own God in prayer several times a day.

When they refused to recognize a man as their god, Nebuchadnezzar ordered all three of them to be thrown into the oven that melted the gold. The soldiers who escorted the young men to the door of the fiery furnace were killed instantly upon opening it. Shadrach, Meshach and Abednego entered by their own volition. When the king looked inside he clearly saw not three, but four men walking through the flames. Startled and amazed he called them back. When Shadrach, Meshach and Abednego emerged from the furnace whole and unharmed, Nebuchadnezzar dropped to his knees to honor the true and living God. Though he battled his pride and strong will, he was a changed man in his final years, as secular history confirms.

Nebuchadnezzar died and was replaced by his son Evil-Murodach who reigned less than two years before his brother-in-law Neriglissar assassinated him and reigned for four years. Three kings ruled the next three years, and the third one, Nabonidus, fled to Arabia when the priests of Marduk protested his allegiance to the moon-god, Sin. In 552 BC his son Belshazzar took over as king of a nation in rapid decline.

King Belshazzar hosted a party for over a thousand of his elite friends at the royal palace banquet hall. In the midst of lewd festivities he called for the golden cups that were taken from the Jewish Temple at Jerusalem and offered a toast to the gods of Babylon. Attendees were stunned when the "finger of God" crackled like lightning in plain sight and etched the words "mene mene tekel parsin" on a wall. The three words denote numbers, weights, and divisions in Aramaic, but none of the king's counselors could interpret their meaning.

The queen recalled that Daniel, known to Babylonians as Belteshazzar, was taken from Judah and had the power to interpret dreams and solve riddles. Belshazzar offered Daniel great wealth and promised to elevate him to the third highest position in his government if he could solve the mystery. Daniel responded bluntly, "I'm not interested in your rewards and accolades, but I'll interpret for you."

Daniel looked at the wall and said, "God has numbered the days of your kingdom and brought it to an end. You have been weighed in the balances and been found lacking. Your kingdom has been divided and given to the Medes and the Persians." Belshazzar died that night and Darius the Mede soon obtained the kingdom.

Daniel shared other vivid apocalyptic visions that conveyed the root struggle between good and evil that persist in the spirit world, on the stage of nations, and in the hearts of individuals. As was and is the case in the human realm of nations and individuals, strength brought power, power yielded success, success bred prominence, prominence ushered in pride, and pride dependably precedes an imminent fall.

36

Daniel in the Lions' Den

Ezekiel the Levite was a direct descendant of Aaron, Eleazar, and Zadok. Thus, he was qualified to become High Priest, but he was a prisoner in a foreign land, and the Temple had been destroyed. At the age of thirty Ezekiel began to prophesy. He foretold Israel's return and resurgence in Canaan. He provided the blueprint that was used to restore the Temple when the nation returned from exile after he died. His vision of dry bones taking on flesh and coming back to life foreshadowed Jews gathering from every land and reconstituting their nation on the world stage in 1948 after centuries of dormancy.

Ezekiel also forecasted the role of Messiah, and emphasized personal accountability over national responsibility in dealing with the problems of sin, alienation, and spiritual death. He spoke of a new covenant that would require a new will and testament to be drawn up between God and Yisra El, people who wrestle with God.

Ezekiel also foresaw a great battle to end civilization as we know it. That vision combined with other prophecies from other sources, including Daniel, composes the theological foundation for eschatology, the study of the end of the present historic age. Although they were contemporaries whose apocalyptic visions and prophecies were eerily similar, Ezekiel and Daniel did not communicate directly and likely did not share information. Ezekiel dwelled in a rural refugee camp among Jewish commoners and Daniel stayed in the palace with Babylonian aristocrats.

Daniel became so well known and highly regarded among his native peers that upon conquering Assyria, Darius the Mede chose him as one of three administrators over 127 provincial governors. As a Jew, he was an outsider, but he proved to be the most diligent and trustworthy administrator in the new cabinet. The king admired Daniel. He was so impressed he eventually announced a plan to promote him as overseer of the whole empire.

Jealous political adversaries tried to discredit Daniel but couldn't find a flaw to exploit. They started a lot of rumors, but nothing stuck. They laid traps with extortion and graft, but he never engaged. Then they realized that the unusual strength he displayed publicly lay in the moral character and personal integrity he derived from his unwavering devotion to God. He prayed continually.

A band of Daniel's rivals appealed to Darius' vanity. They flattered and cajoled him, saying, "Oh great King Darius, the governors agree that you should issue an executive order that all subjects of the land must pay homage to you alone for the next thirty days or be thrown to the lions." They persuaded the king to make a public decree that could not be amended or repealed.

Daniel knew about the decree but routinely went to his room with the windows open toward Jerusalem and prayed to God anyway, just as he had always done. His foes stalked him and confronted him in the midst of his prayers for guidance, courage, and wisdom to govern well and always live an exemplary life. They ran to Darius to confirm the decree and demand that it be properly executed.

Darius gladly received them and assured them he would not back down from his charge. When they informed him they caught Daniel violating the order, Darius became visibly upset. But there was nothing he could do to spare Daniel, whom he favored over all the rest. He couldn't ignore his obligation in front of those he held accountable for carrying out his decrees. He couldn't make an exception and display favoritism to one of their peers. The king made every effort to save Daniel, but in the end he was compelled to issue the inevitable order.

Daniel was seized and brought to a cave where mountain lions dwelt. Darius was apologetic and distraught. Daniel was understanding and compliant. "May your God, whom you serve incessantly, recue you!" Darius uttered to Daniel before the mob shoved him inside the lions' den and rolled a stone over the only entrance. Darius used his signet ring to put his stamp on hot wax that was used to seal the barrier. Then he retired to the palace, where he paced all night and refused to eat or drink, or to talk with anyone.

At dawn Darius returned to the cave and yelled, "Daniel, has the God you persist in serving been able to save you from the lions?" When Daniel answered in the affirmative, the king called for his immediate release, whereupon he had Daniel's accusers rounded up and thrown into the cave along with their family members. Great screaming, roaring and commotion were followed by a dreadful silence deep in the den of contented cats.

Not long after that, Darius threw in with Cyrus the king of Persia and yielded his kingdom. Daniel thrived under the reign of Darius the Mede and continued to serve Cyrus the Persian for another year. What became of Daniel after that is unclear, but he presumably remained in Babylon when the people of Israel were released from bondage and allowed to go home after seventy years in captivity. No mention is made of him in the Jerusalem accounts.

37

Going Home

Whether you choose to call it the providence of God, an obscure coincidence, or an absolutely incredible turn of luck; the brutal Assyrians who captured Israel and harassed Judah were conquered by oppressive Babylonians, who were defeated by more reasonable Medes, who yielded to the accommodating Persians who released the Jews to go back home and rebuild their capital city. The Persians even paid the Jews to reestablish their sacred Temple after seventy years of captivity, exactly as dozens of prophecies written decades beforehand had prescribed with ridiculously accurate timing and precision.

King Cyrus of Persia observed that his expansive Medo-Persian empire which included Libya, Egypt, the northern half of the Sinai Peninsula, much of Europe, virtually all of the Middle East, and parts of what we call India and Russia remained peaceful and strong when he let those he conquered maintain their social, political, and religious order. He did not obliterate cultures because he couldn't tax what he destroyed. He didn't assimilate because intertwining cultures introduced conflicts and compromise that led to tension that demanded resources and oversight. He advocated that happy communities don't revolt. Where possible, Cyrus allowed those he conquered to retain their identity, institutions, and customs, as long as they paid modest taxes and didn't cause trouble for their other neighbors. And he let those who had been displaced or enslaved by prior governments repatriate their homelands.

In 538 BC, not knowing it had been prophesied by Jeremiah long before he rose to power, Cyrus issued what he intended as a self-serving decree. "Cyrus, King of Persia, declares that the God of heaven has given me all the kingdoms of earth and has appointed me to build a temple for him at Jerusalem in Judah. Anyone among you who worships the God of Israel, may his God be with him, is free to go up to Jerusalem in Judah and build this temple of the Lord, the God of Israel, the God who is in Jerusalem. And the residents where survivors may now be living are to provide silver and gold, goods and livestock, and freewill offerings for the temple of God in Jerusalem."

Millions of Jacob's descendants lived in Persian controlled territory. People from the Northern Kingdom of Israel who were taken captive in 722 BC integrated into various societies they landed in. They were established and the vast majority had intermarried, so they stayed where they were. Those who drifted back were not welcomed and accepted by their kinfolk from the Southern Kingdom. Their documents were lost or destroyed so they could no longer certify their ancestral lineage. Those who returned settled in the area around their old capital of Samaria and became known as Samaritans.

In contrast, those who were deported from the Southern Kingdom between 605 and 586 BC kept their scrolls and meticulously maintained their family records in Babylonia and at the refugee city of Tel-Abib where Ezekiel was based. They coveted and protected the scrolls of their laws, prophecies and heritage above everything else. Their pedigrees were intact through Abraham, Isaac, and Jacob, all the way back to Adam.

They rightly called the territory of their ancestors the land of Israel, though the borders they claimed more closely approximated the Southern Kingdom of Judah. Over three fourths of the 42,360 who returned in the first wave had ties to the clan of Judah. Upon their migration back to Jerusalem they became known as Jews. When 652 descendants of Hobaiah, Hakkoz, and Barzillai could not find their family records they were counted as impure and coldly cast out among the Samaritans the purists looked down on.

Cyrus returned the Temple articles Nebuchadnezzar looted to King Jehoiachin's son, Sheshbazzar, who was an infant when his family was deported. Among the twelve leaders appointed to escort the multitude home were Zerubbabel and Nehemiah, whose mention in the Bible documents the physical and emotional weightiness of the nation's homecoming. When they laid the foundation for the Temple it was hard to distinguish the wailing and weeping from the joyous shouts that were heard miles away.

In another curious coincidence, Daniel resurfaced in Babylon with a last great prophesy just as the foundation of the Temple was being put in place. Daniel accurately forecasted that four kings would follow Darius in Persia like Jeremiah accurately forecasted the fall of Nineveh and the obscure rise of an unprecedented shared kingdom of Medes and Persians.

Daniel had previously interpreted Nebuchadnezzar's dream of Medo-Persia, Greece, and Rome that displaced, or grew out of, Babylonia. At this juncture he clearly envisioned Cyrus' empire would be broken up at its peak and parceled out. He foresaw and wrote about the extended conflicts in Egypt and Syria and perfectly described a conquering king of Greece that turned out to be Alexander the Great decades into the future.

He further shared his personal encounter with an angel that was dispatched but delayed for 21 days by demonic spirits that obstructed his passage through the spiritual world that Daniel tapped into by his intense steady prayer. Most significantly, Daniel was shown an image of a great worldly figure in the very distant future who set himself up to displace God. In Daniel's apocalyptic vision this figure won the hearts of people by assuring justice, prosperity, and security for all. He lied to gain power over nations of men and in the middle of his reign unleashed unimaginable oppression and suffering upon the Earth.

He is referred to in Christian theology as Antichrist, the antithesis of a true savior of humanity. When he appears on the world stage he will be the personification of deception, the embodiment of evil, and the prime adversary of Jesus Christ on the material Earth. In Daniel's vision he was ultimately conquered and displaced by the Messiah long foretold in scripture. Given the absolute fulfillment of various prophets' radical visions already, such proposed futuristic events should hold a modicum of credibility even among the most cynical of minds.

38

Rebuilding the Temple

The processional of over forty thousand new Jewish arrivals was stunned when they reached Jerusalem. Aside from a few hundred squatters, the city remained virtually abandoned for seventy years after Nebuchadnezzar laid siege to it. The pilgrims didn't know what they would find, but what they found was not what they expected. The good news was they didn't have to contend with anyone to take back their great capital. The bad news was that it still lay in ruins and was hardly habitable.

Rebuilding the Temple and restoring worship was their first priority, but reconstruction stalled from 535 until 522 BC. The people were excited, but they lacked materials, expertise, guidance, and patience. They piled rocks and lumber that once composed the houses and buildings of their ancestors, and cleared debris that obstructed their passage on deserted streets. Then they got diverted and became preoccupied with making homes and raising crops. Curious pesky neighbors from the surrounding territory also proved to be a distraction.

King Cyrus supported and even promoted their repatriation, but he died in 530 BC and his son, Cambyses, assumed the throne for seven years. He is referred to as Xerxes in the Bible, but Persian records don't list Xerxes among Persia's rulers until much later. Critics used that information to discredit the Bible until archeologists in the last century uncovered that Xerxes was a title before it was used as a name. More often than not, new scientific discoveries confirm the Bible rather than disprove it, especially when context and cultural nuances are uncovered and better understood.

Cambyses, like his father, endorsed the Jews' effort but had other pressing matters to attend to. In 525 BC he led his forces into Egypt to overtake Pharaoh Amasis and his son Psamtik II in Memphis, eliminating a rival and further expanding Persia's territory. That set the stage for Alexander the Great to later conquer the region and impose his Greek culture and language. When the Roman Empire displaced the Greeks and established their orderly governance and infrastructure the stage was set for Messiah.

The Persian kingdom started to unravel while Cambyses was away on a crusade and his aids in the palace assassinated his half-brother, Smerdis, to put down a coup. In 522 BC Guamata the Mede initiated riots and revolt claiming to be Smerdis. The Bible refers to this pseudo-Smerdis as Artaxerxes. Again, this was a title that predated the reign of King Artaxerxes sixty years later. What tripped scholars up was again later documented and clarified.

Cambyses died in a campaign that year and a distant relative named Darius, named after the Mede, stepped in to kill Guamata, squelch the rebellion, and restore order. Haggai the prophet and Zechariah the governor rallied the people in Jerusalem to get serious about restoring the Temple while the Persian government was still amenable.

The project advanced rapidly until Tattenai, who was governor of all the territory west of the Euphrates, and Shethar-Bozenai, who was overseer of the area around Jerusalem questioned by what authority the Jews were building such an elaborate structure in such a defensible location. Jewish leaders appealed to Darius who ordered a search of the records and found Cyrus' original decree.

Darius not only stood up for Israel's right to rebuild the Temple and the city. He compelled Tattenai to pay for it out of the trans-Euphrates treasury, and instructed Shethar-Bozenai not to come around unless he was invited or had something to offer the Jews. That cover inspired the Jews to work diligently and provided clout for them among local antagonists.

Haggai the prophet was obsessed with rebuilding the Temple. Governor Zechariah was obsessed with rebuilding the civil government. It was time to restore proper worship and Zechariah proposed that the nation would only thrive if her people acknowledged God and followed his rules and statutes. He placed a crown on Jeshua, the nation's new head priest, and commissioned him to reinstate traditional feast days and assemble a court of priests to judge the nation according to Mosaic laws.

The crown was a symbol of power vested in the High Priest who oversaw the court of the Sanhedrin. Seventy priests, or clerics, oversaw the administration of justice with a charge to invoke God's righteous will over his people. What started as a commendable act of worship would become a political nightmare when institutional power accrued to self-serving individuals over time, as it always eventually does.

The Temple was completed in the year 516 BC exactly seventy years to the month after it had been destroyed by Nebuchadnezzar in 586 BC. As a side note, the first deportation occurred in 605 BC and the first wave of settlers returned in 535 BC, exactly seventy years later. After the Temple was dedicated the Passover holiday celebration was reinstated and people gathered to sing the very Psalms we read from the Bible today.

39

Queen Esther

Persia in the fifth century BC was grander and more sophisticated than any kingdom before it had ever been. Darius died in 486 BC and left his son, a spoiled brat, to rule. Xerxes was a departure from his predecessors. He had been pampered and protected, so he was emotionally immature, selfish, and undisciplined. Xerxes opened the palace for a national party that lasted six months. Commoners and aristocrats alike ate delicacies that streamed from the royal kitchen and drank choice wine from golden goblets. No one knew how Xerxes was impacting the treasury, nor did they seem to care. To celebrate hosting such a great party, Xerxes held a weeklong private party with his "friends and advisors".

In a drunken stupor, Xerxes summoned his gorgeous wife so he could flaunt her in front of his friends. Not surprisingly, she didn't come. The king was furious. Memucan, a friend and close advisor, submitted that if the king let Queen Vashti get away with such conduct, every woman in the country would show their husbands the same disrespect. The crude and rowdy crowd that surrounded Xerxes persuaded him to make an example of her by replacing her with someone more appreciative and cooperative. Hundreds of beautiful young women were brought in and submitted to a one year beauty regimen that would pale any pageant in the world.

Mordecai was an infant when Nebuchadnezzar uprooted his family from their home in Jerusalem and brought them to Babylon. As a teenager he was selected and trained for duty in the palace like Daniel, Meshach, Shadrach, and Abednego. He was now a royal servant. When Mordecai's brother and sister-in-law died unexpectedly, he adopted their infant daughter and raised her as his own. Hadassah grew to be well poised and stunningly beautiful.

Upon hearing what the king was doing, and how the girls were being pampered, Mordecai introduced the young maiden to his palace friend Hegai who was in charge of the king's haram. Hegai enrolled Hadassah in the grooming process, assigned seven maidens to attend her, and moved her to one of the best suites in the compound. She was introduced as Esther, and no one knew she was a Jew. Not only did her flawless beauty win the favor of her judges, her performance exceeded that of the other contestants because she followed Hegai's instructions to the letter.

She was such an outstanding candidate that she was introduced to the king two months before she completed the grooming program. The king was thrilled. Xerxes crowned Esther queen in place of Vashti and declared a national holiday. On the occasion of her royal intro-duction Mordecai was present and overheard Bigthana and Teresh, two of the king's bodyguards, plotting to assassinate him. He got word to Esther and Esther warned Xerxes. Xerxes confirmed it and had the rebels executed.

Afterward, Xerxes promoted Haman the Ammonite, one of Morde-cai's peers, over all the other palace servants. Everyone started bowing and paying homage to Haman, but Mordecai still called him by his name and refused to bow. Haman was vengeful and determined that instead of taking his rage out on Mordecai he would vent on Morde-cai's entire race, whom the Ammonites despised.

Since Haman now had the king's ear he approached him and said, "There is a peculiar group of people scattered throughout your provinces that refuses to put your laws above their own. For your sake, great king, issue a decree and I will take care of exterminating them wherever they can be found in your kingdom." Haman drafted the decree and Xerxes signed it.

Haman had royal secretaries translate the decree into every known language and sent it out to governors in every province under Persian rule. On the thirteenth day of the twelfth month every Jew, male or female, young or old, was to be assassinated and whoever killed them could legally confiscate their property. Haman built a 75 foot gallows in plain sight on which he intended to personally hang Mordecai. Terror gripped the Jewish population.

When Esther learned what was happening she sent an attendant to check on Mordecai. Mordecai sent back a note begging Esther to intervene with the king on her people's behalf. Esther responded that if she approached the king without being summoned she could be put to death. Mordecai replied, "Do you think you'll be spared when all the other Jews in the land are slain? You alone are in a position to do something. Perhaps this is why you were born."

This was her reply, "Get every Jew you know to pray and fast for me. I and my entourage will do the same. In three days I will approach the king, even though it is against the law. If I must die, I will die."

Esther dressed in royal attire and stood in the doorway of the throne room. When Xerxes saw her he beckoned her to approach and asked her what she wanted. She invited the king to lunch and asked him to bring Haman, who bragged about it to his wife and friends. Xerxes was not aware, and likely didn't care, that Esther and Mordecai were Jewish or that the Jews were the object of Haman's wrath.

Xerxes was perusing official records and realized he never rewarded

Mordecai for his part in apprehending his would be assassins. When he addressed Haman and invited him to lunch, Xerxes asked how he should reward one of the noblest men in the country. Haman, assuming he was that man, recommended the king put his robe on him and let him parade through the city in the king's chariot to the cheers of the people.

Over lunch Esther confronted Haman in front of the king and the king turned the tables on Haman. At Esther's request, Xerxes revised the decree, giving Jews the right to defend themselves against any aggressor and allowing them to kill and plunder their adversaries on the very day set aside for their annihilation. Haman was hanged on the gallows he built for Mordecai and Mordecai was promoted to a rank well above that which Haman had occupied and paraded through the city in the king's chariot. The Jewish holiday of Purim is still practiced today in celebration of that occasion. The Jews are reminded annually that in their most hopeless circumstances they can look for a savior among them to save them and get them through their certain demise. That's why Messiah would be born.

40

Malachi's Rebuke

Upon the death of Haman and the annihilation of thousands of Israel's sworn enemies around 480 BC, life resumed a semblance of normalcy for Jews throughout the Persian provinces. The vast majority of Jews remained in Babylon, but tens of thousands returned to their homeland of Judah under King Darius' authorization. Almost all of them occupied Jerusalem, but a few were drawn to outlying villages they or their ancestors had vacated a century before.

The people of Israel anticipated the arrival of their prophesied Messiah with growing intensity. What an opportune time for someone to arise in their midst and lead them back to prominence, or even dominance, among the nations of the world. As time passed, obligations developed, opposition grew, and zeal diminished.

The Temple was rebuilt and rituals were reinstated. Government was put under the purview of religious leaders, or clerics. Jeshua, the first High Priest of the new order, seated a council of seventy elders comprised of Zadokites, the elite establishment priests, and Pharisees, religious administrators drawn from the ranks of the common merchant class. Not all of them shared Jeshua's piety and devotion. The Council, or Court of the Sanhedrin, became a haven for political operatives with self-serving interests.

The religious institution of the Jews was not unlike the institutional church in our day. Because it hoisted the banner of "God's house" it evoked elevated expectations and respect. Because it was comprised of willful men it was impure and flawed and became the object of disrespect and even disdain. Zadok's descendants were raised in and groomed for the institution. Some were genuinely pious. Almost all were elite scholars and heady aristocrats. They became known as Sadducees.

Pharisees were comparable to lay leaders of today, highly regarded merchants and craftsmen who dedicated themselves to religious pursuits. Coming from a different position they brought fresh insight and a different perspective to interpreting the sacred scriptures and administering "righteous judgment". Sadducees viewed the Council as their privileged profession. The more popular, better liked Pharisees sought guidance from creative inspiration. Both sides struggled to enforce their various genuine aims and objectives. Each found means to impose their cherished positions in the name of God.

Seats of power and influence perpetually changed in Babylon as in Jerusalem. In 465 BC King Xerxes was assassinated and his son Longimanus began to reign as Artaxerxes I. Instability yielded a lack of direction that led to discouragement and cynicism on the part of Jewish commoners. People arrived at the same conclusions people usually come to when their world is in crisis and disarray. "If there is a caring God, why doesn't he intervene?" and worse, "If God doesn't show himself when my need is apparent, maybe there is no God at all."

People in Jerusalem lost faith in their leaders. Commitment diminished. Temple attendance declined. Income dwindled when bureaucrats misappropriated the taxes and tithes they were entrusted with and failed to mete out justice. The Temple fell into disrepair. Half-hearted worshippers brought blemished sacrifices. Immorality infiltrated homes and market places. Jews intermarried with outsiders who worshiped alien gods. Divorce was common. Corruption, perversion and aggression, the pillars of godless civilization were fomenting.

Esther spoke up to save the Jewish nation from extinction at the hands of men. Now Malachi raised his voice to spare the nation from the hand of almighty God. His message was clear and simple, "Look at you. What do you expect?" They were calibrated to the world and reaping the rewards and effects of materialism. To live on a higher plain they needed to recalibrate to a different standard. They needed to repent to the standard their patriarchs were entrusted with. They were chosen and called out to exemplify a godly nation. They were already failing again.

Following in the mold of good King Josiah, Malachi did not call people back to religion but righteousness. Malachi complained about the lack of integrity in the Temple and the moral erosion that gripped the culture. He took priests to task for accepting crippled animals contrary to the law, and for displaying contempt for the Lord that they would never show to their Persian governors. He asked, "If you approached your governors in the same manner you deal with God, how favorably would they treat you?" a stinging rebuke.

Malachi had no institutional authority. He may have been personally frustrated when nothing seemed to change, but his inspired message had been planted. The seed grew roots, produced a stalk, and bore fruit that later changed the nation. Righteous people get discouraged when corruption sets in and wickedness prevails. Like Malachi, they need to remember the book of life has been written from cover to cover and we are simply living out its pages. God is sovereign and his story, history, began and will end according to his plan and purpose whether we ever come to understand and accept it or not.

Every person has a will to direct his own destiny. No man or human institution can subvert the inevitable outcome God established at the onset of his human project. Wisdom dictates that when we see we are off course we need to recalibrate. You can object to that, disregard it, or you can comply. But "I am I am" ultimately dictates, "What is is."

41

Restoring Jerusalem

Zechariah crowned Jeshua as the Head Priest in Jerusalem and Jeshua established a seventy member governing council. Over the years, Jeshua ceded his gavel and new clerics came and went. The national government was in shambles and the lavish Temple was a flop. After several years on the throne of Persia, Artaxerxes had his hands full. The palace was bloated with greedy bureaucrats. Revolts were springing up in outlying provinces. Uncooperative military leaders and regional governors carved out and protected their own niches. Yet Artaxerxes continued to favor the Jews.

Ezra, a prominent descendant of Levi, Aaron, and Zadok, held the necessary qualifications of a Head Priest according to his heritage, though he never assumed the role formally. He approached Artaxerxes concerning his struggling brethren in Jerusalem and the king sanctioned millions of dollars in aid and supplies and provided a letter directing local governors to give Ezra whatever he needed in order to rebuild and reestablish Jerusalem.

Ezra, already regarded among Israelites as a great teacher and their most distinguished expert in Mosaic law, left Babylon in 458 BC with 1500 Levites he interviewed and screened for their dedication to restoring the Temple. It took several months and when he arrived at Jerusalem he was appalled. Hundreds of matters needed to be addressed, but one stood above everything else. Looking for a common link to national success and failure, Ezra established a single simple priority.

Government was not it. Different modes yielded varied results and all led to corruption and brokenness. Education was not it. What people know doesn't always translate into what they do. Religion wasn't it. Ezra was staring at evidence of willful abuse all around him. Every organization and institution Ezra considered was prone to compromise and corruption, but one served as a barometer and rose to indicate the course of a nation. When it fails a nation falls. If men will not commit to preserving the health and wellbeing of their families, even at their own peril and expense, no other institution can hold a nation together for long.

Ezra observed that cross-cultural intermarriage led to rampant divorce. He came to understand that when personal desire trumps communal interest, people compromise to the point of submission or indifference. He wisely surmised that until the nation of Israel shared a devotion to the traditional Jewish family's welfare and security, no enterprise could withstand the unavoidable unsolicited trials of life more than a few generations. That's why Jews diligently preserve and utilize their family ties today.

Joshua admonished his generation, "Choose this day whom you will serve. But as for me, and my house, we will serve the Lord." Elijah confronted the prophets of Baal, then turned to his clan and pled, "How long will you halt between two opinions. If Baal is to be your god, then follow his ways. But if you would follow God, commit to live his way."

Ezra stood before his faltering nation and heralded them to repent yet again and recalibrate to the benchmark of their sacred Deity.

The sanctified scholar demanded allegiance to the sacred scrolls, noting that even priests married people that recognized different customs and pursued different goals based on what or whom they worshipped. If they would be "the people of God", the Jews had to dedicate themselves to God. Their primary allegiance to God dictated who they could marry. Ezra demanded that sincere Jews either leave their unbelieving spouses or stay married to an unbelieving spouse and leave Jerusalem.

Israel was at a crossroads and the situation was dire. Ezra would sooner die than let the nation perish again. There would be no more infidelity, promiscuity, perversion, prostitution, or compromise. It had to start at home. And so it did. Pain brought progress at home and beyond.

Fourteen years after sponsoring Ezra, Artaxerxes noticed that his devoted Jewish cupbearer, Nehemiah, seemed sad. Upon the king's inquiry Nehemiah shared that his brother reported progress in Jerusalem had halted. Local provincial governors, jealous Samaritans, and internal saboteurs frustrated Ezra and thwarted construction.

The king appointed his trusted servant and longtime loyal friend to be interim governor of the region. In 445 BC Nehemiah joined Ezra in Jerusalem to squelch the opposition. New walls were built and the city was fortified within six months. There wasn't enough room for the Jewish population that now numbered in the hundreds of thousands inside the walls of Jerusalem so Nehemiah crafted a plan to redistribute the population that made the people happy and the city strong.

On what has since been recognized as the first day of the Jewish civil year Ezra, Nehemiah, and the Levites called a solemn assembly and began a public reading and interpretation of the Torah scroll. Over a three week span the nation's spirit was broken as they devoted themselves to systematically considering what was actually contained in what is the foundation of our modern Bible.

Nehemiah remained governor of Israel in Judah for eleven years before he returned to the service of Artaxerxes in the Persian capital of Susa. Those he left in charge allowed corruption to seep back into Jewish culture. Some even married outsiders and allowed them to worship their pagan gods. Nehemiah was furious. He told the king he had neglected to properly dedicate the walls of Jerusalem and asked for permission to return. Nehemiah returned to Jerusalem in 432 BC. Insulated by his authority as the personal emissary of the distant king who superseded the rule of those who governed the Temple, he confronted the priests, took them to task and whipped them back into shape, much like a better known figure that would follow in his steps four centuries later.

Nehemiah came down hard on those who defiled the Temple, perverted the law of God, and led others astray. Only after Nehemiah reformed the government and reestablished righteous devotion did he commence with dedicating the wall he would forever be known for reconstructing. Nehemiah learned that any barrier to danger outside must be diligently monitored and preserved by righteousness on the inside. A strong city has both a solid wall and a righteous Temple.

42

Old Testament Overview

The age of the universe, or even Earth, is irrelevant to understanding the Bible. It is enough to recognize a vast world exists in a physical form where mankind sojourns on a distinct planet in a peculiar solar system in a particular galaxy. Everything concerning how or when we got here is superfluous.

The first couple of chapters of the Bible offer a brief synopsis of the genesis of a material world birthed from a pre-existent non-material source. More than ancient manuscripts, what we have come to call the Old Testament is sacred text supernaturally preserved so individual men can understand and react to their spiritual essence in a material world.

Coming from different points of view, scientists and theologians converge on the logical notion that all substance appeared from nothing at all in immediate compliance with and ongoing conformance to all the immutable laws that govern natural science today. At some point, life emerged to animate physical objects. Later animated physical beings obtained increasing levels of intelligence. Man alone was eventually infused with the very Spirit of the pre-existent non-material source we recognize as God.

Men have the intellectual capacity to speculate, but we have no prehistoric records. History, by definition, began when men started sharing and recording their observations, assumptions, and speculations. From Old Testament records, that happened 5777 to 6282 years ago. Many secular sources expand the "historical" account by as much as 2000 years, but each passing year new discoveries and continuing analysis better reconcile with the Biblical perspective. By the time we have a firm date, the Bible suggests time will be no more.

In the course of six thousand years or so, the scripted story of man has unfolded as outlined in an amazing treatise composed by more than forty contributing authors who spanned over 1600 years and had no way of coordinating their efforts. The last four to five thousand years of Biblical history have proven quite dependable and are increasingly recognized as accurate.

However, as stated in the beginning of this book, the Bible nowhere purports to be a science or history textbook. The Bible is an operating manual to help those who espouse faith in the Bible's professed source of our creation to navigate through a material world on a spiritual journey.

The spiritual bond that initially tethered man to God was, and is, severed when man invokes his free and independent will. We are taught in the earliest chapters of the Bible that material enterprises are made to conform to spiritual intent, not the other way around. God "wrote the book", so He knew and made accommodation for man's deviance. Adam was banished from his original state in the garden paradise, but assured of ultimate restoration.

Given over to his own pursuits, man drifts ever deeper into debauchery. God illustrated His tolerance to the point of judgment and remedy. Noah was saved and assigned to replenish and oversee the Earth in order to preserve and expand God's physical domain.

What was salvaged was again corrupted. Willful men abused resources and perverted nature. God called a righteous man from the midst of wayward society. Abraham left his family, friends, and familiar surroundings to establish an exemplary nation in a hostile environment. But Abraham and his descendants were beset by impatience and lack of discipline. They succumbed to material leanings.

Willful spiritual disobedience led to worldly oppression and bondage, but God miraculously orchestrated events to right the course of his obstinate "chosen people". Moses communed with God and followed God's instruction to lay down His laws for human conduct. Moses led Earth-bound people back to their promised abode. Every person who would live in God's domain on Earth now has access to the tools, resources, and instructions necessary to live in righteous accord. As the Apostle Paul later concluded, "The law was given to showcase that men can't abide there on their own for long."

Failing to follow through on God's command to purge themselves and their surroundings of evil influence, the entire race faltered and fell from grace yet again. At odds with God and each other, God raised up a mighty king for his people. But David too succumbed to carnal frailty. An aspiring righteous clan ascended to dominate the Levant only to fall to greater worldly powers and was again subjected to oppression and bondage.

Miracles and prophesies abound throughout the latter period encouraging believers who then lived, and now read, through the Old Testament. From the onset in the Garden of Eden, God incubated his plan of redemption.

Old Testament stories show us that man was made by and for God for a purpose beyond our full comprehension. They reveal a pattern whereby men who were created by and for God incessantly draw away from spiritual influence in pursuit of physical gratification. And they portray a gracious father figure who allows his children to exercise foolish immature discretion in the hope and with the expectation they will eventually grow up and gain a more suitable and sustainable perspective aligned with his good intention toward them.

That intention is revealed in the New Testament. To understand the full plan of salvation depicted in the Bible, one must read the whole story of man's projected course on a distinct planet in a peculiar solar system in a particular galaxy in a vast universe where material existence is directed by a pre-existent creative spiritual force. The God of the Bible will ultimately prevail and make Himself known. He has a particular aspiration for you that you will be wise to entertain. It's in the Bible. Keep reading. Start praying. Keep searching. "He that seeks, will find."

CPSIA information can be obtained
at www.ICGtesting.com
Printed in the USA
LVOW10s0619180717

541720LV00001B/271/P

9 780998 182957